YOU AND ADULTS

YOU AND ADULTS

by
Lawrence O. Richards

MOODY PRESS
CHICAGO

Printed in the United States of America

Contents

Part 1
PRINCIPLES

1

Teaching for Transformation

It was a review session, yet one of the most exciting adult classes I've seen. During the past three weeks, we had explored together the Bible's teaching that man was created "in the image of God" (Gen. 1:26-27). Today, we started off in a simple way, listing on the chalkboard "Key Truths":

      1. We're special to God.
         (Gen 1:26-27; Gen 2)
      2. We were created for God.
         (Col 1:16; Gen 1—dominion)
      3. We're invited to obey.
         (Gen 3; Jn 14:15)

Then we went around the circle, each of us telling which of these truths seemed most important to us. For Joan, it was the first: we're special. Pat was impressed with the third area, that somehow obedience is for blessing rather than a harsh demand. Ray had felt this too. For Connie, the second area of truth seemed most meaningful.

When everyone had expressed himself in general terms, we added another column to the chart on the board: "What response have we made to these truths?"

The responses

At this point, our class became exciting—now that we could clearly see that God was actively working in us!

Joan

In our first session on the image of God, we began by sharing. Each of us in the circle of about twelve adults gathered at the Y across the street from our church told "one thing you really like about yourself." For some it was hard! Joan particularly had hesitated in embarrassment, then with a smile said that she really didn't know anything she liked about herself. Others had dodged the question, and said such things as: "I like the fact that I can pray and know God will hear me." "I like sunny days." But Joan's response had been painful and honest. Later that morning, Joan shared some of the reasons for her hesitation.

After our opening sharing, we went on to note that God said, "Let us make man in our image" only of man. We had seen that even after the fall, the image and likeness remained (Gen 9:6; Ja 3:9). Each of us then read Genesis 2 individually, to find and share evidences from the Bible text that God had shown special interest in Adam. We saw that every possible human need (physical, emotional, spiritual, and social) had been planned for by God as He shaped creation to provide for this crown of His workings.

And then we began to dig deeper into the subject. How might Adam have felt to realize that he was truly special to God? How does it make us feel to realize that *we* are special to Him too?

It was here that Joan shared more. When she was being brought up, her dad was afraid she'd become a superficial and proud person. So he made sure she wouldn't! For instance, when Joan would glance in a mirror, he would say, "You don't need to look in a mirror to see if you're beautiful. I'll tell you if you're beautiful"—and he never did! Joan had grown up convinced that she was not special at all; that in fact, she was very ordinary, of very little worth. The idea that she was really special, special to God as a unique person, made in His image and tremendously valuable to Him, was a jolt.

That was why I was so excited about that review session. As we talked of our response to the truths we'd been studying, Joan told how God had literally turned around her feelings about herself. That first Sunday morning, she had realized for the first time that she *was* valuable. And during the week that followed, the Lord had shown her in three distinct ways that she truly was special to Him. Now, a month later, Joan accepted and liked herself. And she was a different mother, seeking ways to help her young children feel good about themselves as special people, conscious of and avoiding the mistakes her parents had made in rearing her.

Through a study of the Word of God, Joan's inner perceptions and attitudes had changed, and her behavior had changed too!

Pat and Ray

Pat's the quiet type—big, gentle, thoughtful, calm. Ray's different. He was brought up in a home where work and performance were given great emphasis. And he's driven hard all of his life. In fact, he has felt uncomfortable when he wasn't active, trying to accomplish some task. Both these men reported that day that they had been particularly impressed with the third truth: we're invited to obey.

We had begun that class with a lecture, organized around the thought expressed in John 14:15: "If you love Me, you will keep my commandments." I had pointed out that the Bible constantly associates love and obedience, both from the point of view that God's motive for insisting on obedience is His love for us, and that it is only love for God (*not* knowledge of what's right) that moves us to obey Him. Then we had looked together into Genesis 3, to see how God's love for Adam and Eve had been expressed and why our first parents had disobeyed.

This too had involved much sharing. We recalled how we had felt about commands given by different people in our experience. We talked together about our own children, and discussed how we could communicate standards to them in a way that the love would come through.

What had this study meant to Pat and Ray during the week that followed? Pat shared that it had made him more sensitive to his children, and that he had consciously tried new ways to help them respond. Ray told of a couple of incidents during the week when he had been sensitive to the Holy Spirit's promptings. "I used to think such feelings were silly, and work harder at whatever I was doing. But it seemed to me that since God *invites* us to obey in a loving way, He wouldn't be hitting me over the head. So when I felt Thursday that God wanted me to stop and take a ride with a friend (I usually like to drive my own car), I did it—and we shared some important things. What it boils down to, I guess, is that I don't feel the pressure to 'prove myself' like I did."

Connie

Our second class had begun with sharing too. I'd written Colossians 1:16 on the chalkboard: "By him were all things created . . . all things were created by him, and for him" (KJV). Underneath I'd written an incomplete sentence. "I was created for Jesus to—" Our launching was to go around the class and share one thing each of us felt he was created to do or be for Jesus.

The class came up with quite a list! To praise Him; to glorify Him; to worship Him; to be a good father; to do good to others; to trust Him; to enjoy life; to be thankful.

Then I quickly sketched from Genesis 1 the portrait of God shaping our world, with all His work culminating in man. Man was not only made in God's image and likeness as a person, but was even given dominion. It was exciting to see. God, who made all things by and for Jesus Christ, entrusted them into our hands. It was given us to enjoy, and to take care of for Him. There were some thoughts on ecology, but the most important thought we focused on was this: If *dominion* carries with it the idea of "care for" even more strongly than "control"—how exciting to realize that you and I are under Christ's dominion. He commits Himself to care for us, who were made *for* Him.

This truth had been real to Connie these past weeks, as she had found it another encouragement to relax and trust the Lord in everything. During the review class, she shared, "Everything used to have to be so exact for me. I had to have just the right kind of drapes, and the right furniture, and my special kind of car, and I was really compulsive about all these things. And you know, since we've lost all that, I've been learning to be satisfied and really happy with the Lord. It's so neat to realize that He actually is taking care of me, and to be able to trust Him."

The excitement

I probably overuse the word *exciting*. But to me, this captures and expresses what it means to teach the Bible to adults.

It's exciting to see God work.

It's exciting to see transformation taking place.

It's exciting to hear people share their experience of God's Word.

These things are exciting to me because they pretty well express the goal I have in teaching. I'm eager for God to be at work in people, transforming them as they experience His Word. I believe this is the goal that each of us who teaches the Word of God must have: we dare not be satisfied with anything less.

God working

As Joan shared the change in her deepest attitudes about herself and the changes this in turn made in her as a mother, I was thrilled and thankful. God was clearly at work in her! As Ray talked of his changed feelings, the same thrill came. God was at work in him! God, who inspired His Word, had used it *today* to touch the lives of these children of His.

This is the first conviction I have to have as I plan to teach the Bible to adults: that God intends to use His Word in their lives, that God is eager to be at work.

Too often when we come to teaching the Bible, our goal unconsciously shifts from eagerness to see God work to other good but inadequate goals, such as: "To help my students understand that—"; or, "To be sure my students know—". Knowledge and understanding are important, of course. But they are just first steps toward the real goal of teaching. Coming to *know* what the Bible says is only one step in opening up our lives to God that He might work freely in us.

Transforming

This is the second conviction I have in teaching adults. Every Christian's life needs more and more of the touch of God. Each believer has the capacity for growth and change.

Sometimes books on teaching adults include chapters describing what they are like. These chapters try to prove that, no matter how old, adults can and need to learn, that adults can grow and change. Or that adults have problems the Bible can speak to.

But we all know these things. The adult education movement involves millions in special courses and training. Even retirement communities provide classes and training sessions. Even more significantly, we know that the Bible says that God seeks to make His children more and more like their heavenly Father (Mt 5:48). We are called to bear the family resemblance of His Son (Ro 8:29), and to be holy as He is holy (1 Pe 1:16). This is possible because, having been born again, we share God's own "indestructible heredity" (1 Pe 1:23, Phillips). The new life that God plants within the believer is to grow throughout his lifetime, that he might become progressively more and more like the Lord.

Whatever the characteristics of an age-group, every adult believer has the potential and need for continuing transformation. Every non-Christian who may be in our class has the potential of conversion and, following this, lifelong growth.

When I approach teaching, then, I come to my class with an expectation that as God works through His Word, my students and I will change!

Experiencing the Word

This final conviction is also basic. I want to teach the Word as something to be experienced—not merely understood. Jesus constantly emphasized this: "Keep my words." He explained the difference between wise and foolish men. The wise hear His words and do them; the foolish hear His words, but do not do them (Mt 7:26-27). It is only as my adult students see the meaning of the Word for their lives and step out in faith to *do* that Word that transformation will take place. It is then we see the reality of God at work in one another, and know the thrill of teaching.

The teacher

Teaching for transformation is exciting, but it is also challenging. It's far more than talking enthusiastically about what the teacher had learned as he studied the Bible in preparation for class (which is what most "lecture" classes for adults involve). It's totally different than simply "communicating." If I am to teach for transformation and for experience of the Word, then there are a number of things I must be concerned with. As a Bible teacher, I need to answer the following questions:

1. How do I help my students to discover the relationship of God's Word to their own lives?

2. How do I help my students *want* to respond to God?

3. How do I communicate the Word clearly, without making the class simply content-centered (a learning of information without impact on life)?

4. How do I help my students grow in the faith needed to step out and trust God in obedience?
5. How do I help my students explore their own attitudes and feelings and behavior in order to bring these into harmony with God's revealed will?
6. How do I plan classes in which God's Spirit is free to touch each student and meet individual needs?

It is questions like these that this little book is designed to explore. And it is with results like those in the lives of Joan and Ray and Connie that we are going to be concerned!

In order to see such results consistently, I am convinced that the teacher *must* plan and teach a participation class. So in this book, I'm going to describe and suggest a distinctive "participation approach" to teaching adults. If you are simply looking for hints on better ways to lecture, you can put this book down now. But if you are looking for a better way to cooperate with God in communication of His *transforming* Word, then read on. In chapters 2-5 we'll examine principles underlying this kind of teaching. In chapters 6-8, we'll explore skills a teacher needs to develop for transformation teaching. And in the final chapters, we'll evaluate ways adult classes may be structured.

Throughout it all, we will focus on how *you* can be a more effective teacher of adults as you join me in teaching for transformation.

REACT

1. I shared some of the specific results of God's work in the lives of adults I taught during the month before this book was begun. List similar evidences of God's work in the lives of the students you taught— this past month.
2. Do you agree or disagree that we should teach adults the Bible "for transformation"?

ACT

1. In the first book of this series, **You, the Teacher,** I discussed the nature of teaching. You may want to read it before going on in this book, as it contains concepts not explored here.

2. A list of questions about teaching adults is found on pages 15-16. Decide which seem most important to you. What would you add to them?

2

A Demonstration Class

In the chapters in this section, we're going to look not at the skills involved in teaching for transformation, but at some of the basic principles on which you and I can structure the teaching situation. We'll examine skills in some detail in Part 2 (chaps. 6-8). But first, we need to discover the underlying principles that give us direction and purpose as we develop skills.

In this chapter, I want to describe a class session that we can refer back to in chapters that follow. This class session demonstrated some of the principles we'll explore. I've chosen a setting that you may find more typical (and far more difficult) than the class I referred to in the first chapter. That class, of around twenty people, is one I teach every week. The class described in this chapter is a group of over two hundred, meeting in a church sanctuary, composed of people who are *not* used to sharing or participating. Yet this class too is designed to involve the learner in ways that open him up to God's Word and to transformation by God's Spirit.

So let's look together at a class we'll refer to often in the next chapters, and see how we can teach the Bible for transformation in *any* situation.

TEACHER (*smiling, and enthusiastic*): Good morning! Say, before we begin, turn to your neighbor, say hello, and tell him or her, "God loves you" this morning. (*Waits.*)

Great! Let's pray as we begin. (*Leads brief prayer.*)

This morning, we're going to probe something that's very familiar to us, yet utterly basic in our lives. It's something we can't get along without as Christians (*pauses*), something we all want to experience more deeply. This is something that Jesus put first in the last supper talk with His disciples, just before the crucifixion. Here's what He said, recorded in John 13:34-35. (*Reads these verses aloud.*) "A new commandment I give to you, that you love one another, even as I have loved you, that you also love one another. By this all men will know that you are My disciples, if you have love for one another."

(*Addresses group.*) Now, if I were just going to lecture on these verses, I'd probably want to make three central points. I'm not going to lecture; I'm going to make you work instead. (*Smiles.*) But if I were to lecture, I'd probably stress these things (*holds poster up with three points outlined*):

1. "This is a new commandment." It's not "new" because it's about love. We've always been told to love our neighbor as ourselves. It's new because it involves a relationship between disciples, between fellow believers. And it's new because this love is to go *beyond* loving as we love ourselves to loving just as Jesus loves us!

2. "This is just as love." When we think about Jesus' love for us, we get many images. But one comes through that is utterly clear. To Jesus, love meant becoming totally involved with His loved ones. He left the glories of heaven and became a human being to share our lot. He reached out to us with His love and became involved. You simply can't love as Jesus loved and not reach out to other people.

3. "Love is the mark of discipleship." Jesus said "all men" would know that we are His disciples when we love one another. Our relationship to Jesus is demonstrated within and outside the church by loving each other just as Jesus loves.

Now, this is what I would talk about if I were to lecture this class. But, as I said, this is going to be a working class. Because what we want to do is to focus on this word that Jesus uses—*love*—and see if we can discover what it really means for our lives. In fact, we want to both understand and experience Jesus' kind of love this morning. So let's begin.

First, turn to your neighbor, and in sixty seconds, come up with a definition of love. (*Gives the adults about a minute and a half, then calls time and hears reports. Writes down on a chalkboard the definitions as given—at least phrases and words that catch their meaning.*)

All right, let's hear some of those definitions (*not bothered by hesitations; simply waits or says something encouraging*).

STUDENT 1: Love is unselfishly caring for another person.

TEACHER: Good (*records "unselfish caring"*). Let's have another.

STUDENT 2: Love is putting others first, yourself second.

STUDENT 3: Love is doing things for others when it costs you something.

STUDENT 4: Love is kind.

STUDENT 5: Love is the capacity to feel deeply with another person and empathize.

STUDENT 6: Love is getting involved with other people to do them good.

STUDENT 7: Love is more a decision of the will than a feeling.

TEACHER: Got a couple more?

STUDENT 8: Love is having God's attitude toward people.

STUDENT 9: Love is something only the Holy Spirit can give you.

STUDENT 10: Love is the most important quality a person can have.

TEACHER: Great! That's quite a list—some real good definitions of love. Now, these are good definitions. But they're what we might call lexical definitions. They explain a word by using other words. There's another kind of definition that helps us get an even deeper understanding. It's called an operational, or behavioral, definition. Instead of using other words to explain what a thing means, this kind of definition explains by showing what that thing does. (*Pauses.*) For instance, when I was a kid, we used to go to Upper Michigan fishing, and lived in a cabin there. In the kitchen was something I really liked. It was a thing that when I made a handle go up and down (*demonstrates pumping motion*), water came out. What was it?

STUDENTS (*several*): A pump.

TEACHER: Right! Now, what I just gave you was an operational definition of a pump. It's something that when you make the handle go up and down, water comes out. I could have given you a definition in words, but you got the idea better and probably quicker than if I'd used a lexical, "explaining" approach. Now, what I want you to do this time is confer with your partner again, and develop at least three operational definitions of love. Tell what love does, not what love is. For instance you might say, "Love is turning off your favorite TV program to listen to your child tell about what he learned in science class." Or, "Love is being the first out of bed to turn up the heat." Take about three minutes, and see what you come up with.

(*Teacher sits down to show that students are on their*

own; after three or four minutes, calls time to hear reports.) All right. Time's up, and I can hardly wait to hear your definitions.

STUDENT 1: Love is listening to someone who needs to talk. *(Teacher nods, smiles, and records this and the following suggestions on the chalkboard.)*

STUDENT 2: Love is hugging your wife.

STUDENT 3: Love is noticing someone looks sad and stopping to talk with them.

STUDENT 4: Love is taking a friend shopping when you're busy.

STUDENT 5: Love is praying for a person who shares a need right then instead of promising to pray later.

TEACHER: That's important, isn't it?

STUDENT 6: Love is spanking your children.

STUDENT 7: Love is telling another person when something he says hurts you.

TEACHER: Yeah.

STUDENT 8: Love is letting someone comfort you.

STUDENT 9: Love is saying I'm sorry as soon as you know you've hurt someone.

STUDENT 10: Love is telling someone thank you.

(When all who want to have shared and their contributions have been recorded on the chalkboard, the teacher continues.)

TEACHER: Very good. I think you can see why the operational definition is important. We get so used to words that we sometimes forget we have to translate them into specific and practical actions to grasp their real meaning.

Actually, one reason the operational definition of love is so important is that this is the kind of definition the Bible uses. We can see some of God's operational definitions by remembering that command, "Love one another." Then if we look in Scripture and locate references to "one another," we get a pretty striking picture of the way Christians are to live with and love each other.

For instance, here are a few of the Bible's definitions of love in action. Romans 14:1 and 15:7 say that we are to "receive one another." Another word for that is to welcome, to accept. I have a friend in Phoenix who visited a church where he was impressed by the friendliness. Half a dozen people met him after the services, shook hands, and said how glad they were to see him. So he went back, and it was the same that week too. Again at least six new folks went out of their way to meet him. So he went back again. But after six weeks, he realized something. He'd been given a friendly welcome—but he still didn't *know* anyone at the church. And then he found out that the people who had been so friendly were assigned to be friendly. They were the church greeters! (*Pauses.*)

Well, that's *not* what this passage is talking about. To welcome means to open up your heart and your life—to invite another person to share with you. And Romans 14 warns us not to do it just to change him or his way of thinking, or just to get him to join the church. We're to welcome one another because we care—because our brother is important to us as a person.

Hebrews 10:24 adds another behavioral description. "Provoke one another," [KJV] is what it says. No, that doesn't mean to get each other mad. It means literally to "stimulate" or "encourage." We used to talk about these things when I was teaching at Wheaton, and some of the students took it seriously. They said, "Hey, let's get together and learn how to love and help each other." I remember one of the girls telling about it later. She'd shared how upset she was because her prayer life wasn't what she wanted. She wanted to spend more time with the Lord, but things kept getting in the way.

So the next day on campus one of the group met her and said, "Hey, how was your prayer time this morning?" Well, it had been pretty bad. So she wasn't sure just what to say. And that afternoon, another one of the group met her in class, and wouldn't you know it, "How'd it go?" All that week different students would ask her how her prayer times were going, and she told me what a tremendous stimulus that was to getting down to pray. So this is part of loving one another too. To care enough about what's happening in another person's life that you ask them, and encourage them, and let them *know* you care.

Galatians 6:2 tells a familiar one. "Bear ye one another's burdens [KJV]." This means two things: when another person shares something with you, you care enough to pray and do whatever's needed to help out. But it also means we need to share our burdens with others. We need to let people know where we're hurting, so they can help. I'm really excited about our church, because this kind of thing is happening. I remember when a former student called and asked me to visit her brother who had tried to commit suicide and was in a hospital. I visited several times and spent hours with him, but then I had to go away on one of my trips. So, at our sharing time at church, I asked folks to pray for Danny. Afterward, three people came up and asked me what his room number was. They weren't only going to pray, they were going to visit him. It was really great to know that others cared enough to actually pick up that burden with me.

It's things like this that let us know the kind of love Jesus wants operating in *our* relationships, right here in our church. We need to ask ourselves, Do I have other people who I know love me, who I know so well that I actually go and share needs and burdens with? Do

I have the kind of relationship with other Christians that makes them feel free to come to me and share their burdens? Is this happening? Well, this is the kind of thing that Jesus makes possible for us, and that is to mark our lives together as His disciples! But there's another kind of definition of love we need to look at. This is an experiential definition. It tells how we experience love. Actually, it's not enough to do things out of love. You have to communicate love in such ways that other people can feel it. For instance, for ten years I used to get up early Saturdays and clean the house for my wife. She's allergic to house dust. So, out of love, I'd do all the cleaning. Then I'd get her up and take her on a tour of our spotless house. Well, after ten years, I found something out. Every one of those tours had been horrible for her, and felt just like a kick in the stomach. You see, she hadn't seen them as a love gift. What she'd felt was shame that she wasn't able to do what a housewife is supposed to do!

So when we start thinking of love, we have to come to know others so well that what we communicate to them is really love. So (*pauses*), ready to work again? (*Pauses.*) You and your partner and another pair talk in a group of four, and share with each other. Here's what to share. Tell each other about one time when you really felt loved and cared for. Try to help each other enter into that experience with you. Really understand what communicated love to you. You've got about eight or ten minutes.

(*When time is up, or sooner if the groups seem to run out of things to share, call time and continue.*)

TEACHER: We've begun to see today a little bit of what love and loving one another means. Love isn't some abstract concept "out there." Love is a practical expression of caring, of getting involved. The fact that Jesus stressed love at that last supper, and that the Bible talks so much about love for one another, tells us something. It tells us that love is a basic need for each of us: that as Christians we *need* to be loved by one another and to love back. We simply won't grow as persons or as Christians without love.

So, as we end our class, I want you to do just one more thing. Back in your groups of four, share with each other this one thing. Where do I most need to be loved just now? What's my greatest need for love and support? And when you've each shared, just take a few minutes to pray for each other. Right now, take time to share. Close in prayer in your group of four, and feel free to leave when you're done. Then class will be over.

REACT

1. How do you think you would have felt if you were a member of this class? Why?
2. How was the concluding activity (sharing needs and praying together in groups of four) related to the lesson as a whole? Why do you suppose the teacher ended class this way?
3. Read through the chapter again, and jot down notes on what seems most important to you about the class structure and process.

ACT

1. Estimate the amount of time the teacher was talking, and the amount of time the students were involved in some kind of participation.
2. Evaluate: how did the teacher attempt to move the talk of love from an idea or con-

cept discussion to a discussion of things that were important to the learners?
3. Evaluate: how was the Bible used in this class? What specific things were communicated? What methods were used? What was "different" about the use of the method(s) here?
4. Write out a brief outline of the last adult class you taught. How, specifically, was it similar to the class described in this chapter? How, specifically, did it differ?

3

Involve Your Students

From the things I shared in the first chapter about my regular class, I'm sure you received an impression of active student involvement. It is a class where everyone is free to share, a place where participation is free and spontaneous. But many adult teachers who *want* participation object when I describe the class. "I've been trying to get involvement," they say, "but my students just won't participate. How do I get involvement?"

That's why I described the larger class, taught to students who are not used to participation, that is transcribed as chapter 2: to demonstrate a basic fact. You *can* have meaningful participation, even in the most difficult of settings! We'll examine some of the skills that help stimulate quality participation in chapters 6-8. But before we think of specific answers to the question of how to get involvement, we need to be very clear about what kind of involvement is helpful in an adult class, and what are the purposes of involvement in teaching the Bible. It's these basic questions, questions of principle, that we want to discuss in this chapter.

Kinds of involvement

"Participation" should never be an end in itself when teaching adults the Bible. The Christian teacher has a unique goal in teaching God's Word. He is teaching for transformation, seeking to help learners open up all their lives to God's Spirit as He communicates to them through His Word. Sometimes, participation gets in the way rather than helps achieve this goal.

Purposeless involvement

One kind of involvement that hurts rather than helps is that with no purpose. "What shall we talk about today?" may seem to indicate openness to students' needs and interests. But it may indicate only a failure to prepare, or a lack of commitment to *Bible* teaching. The meandering "rap session" or "discussion class" popular at times with younger adults soon flags in interest and falls short of bringing learners to the Word with a commitment to learn to do all that the prophets have spoken.

One principle we can state, then, is this: never try to get participation just for the sake of having people participate. Participation should be an integral part of the structure and plan of the lesson, and have a clear relationship to the Bible truth being taught.

Superficial involvement

Superficial involvement *is* related to Scripture, yet that still does not help you move toward the goal of transformation. This is participation that deals with the Bible merely as interesting ideas; that talks of facts and theories, but dodges sharing what the relationship is of God's Word to life.

In one of my classes recently, we were exploring God's concern for people as expressed in the careful design of creation. We saw in Genesis 2 how God had not only met man's physical needs, but also his need for work and a sense of accomplishment (keeping the garden), his need for independent responsibility (dominion, naming the animals), his need for an intimate personal relationship (Adam and Eve were given each other). As we began to explore the implications all this has for us who are, like Adam, made in God's image, one

of my students said, "Personally, I think the automobile companies should do more about pollution than they are doing.
And if man is supposed to be in charge of his world for God,
they certainly ought to accept their responsibilities for—"

Yes, there are ecological implications to these early Genesis
chapters. And we talked about some of them—as they related to *us* and *our* lives. But my friend's several minute
discussion of the responsibilities of automobile companies
and of the impersonal "they" who weren't doing as much
about pollution as they might, led us away from interacting
with the Bible as God's Word to *us*. And this is critical. We
are not studying the Bible to find out how *others* ought to
live in harmony with God and His will. We, as Christians,
are looking into the Word to hear Him speak to us, so that
we might respond in faith and bring our lives into harmony
with Him.

Superficial involvement again, is any involvement that
deals with the Scripture merely as ideas or concepts to talk
of without relationship to our lives. Certainly at times, discussion will center on a Bible concept in order to understand
it as a prelude to applying it. This happened when lexical
and operational definitions of love were developed in the
class reported last chapter. But the point is that those dis-
cussions were part of the overall structure of the class; they
were part of a process designed to lead to a deeply personal
interaction with the Word.

This leads us then to a second principle about participation. Participation that treats Scripture as concepts or ideas
unrelated to the learner's life should not be encouraged,
except when such discussion is part of a process that leads
to personal application of the truth discussed.

Meaningful involvement

Meaningful involvement is what all teachers need to work
toward. This involvement opens lives to the Spirit of God
and the Word of God through which He speaks. What makes

participation meaningful is that it in fact helps the whole class move toward understanding the impact of God's Word on their own lives, and then helps them find freedom to respond to the Word in wholehearted obedience.

Several things characterize meaningful involvement and help a teacher evaluate whether what is going on in a class is helpful or not. So let's look at several qualities of meaningful involvement.

1. It engages the whole person. This is in contrast to the superficial kind of involvement mentioned above. Superficial involvement deals with the Bible as ideas, isolated from life. Meaningful involvement includes expression of feelings, attitudes, values, and experiences of the adults, rather than just thoughts or beliefs.

For example, notice how the class in chapter 2 moved from a lexical definition of love (intellectual level) to an operational definition (involving the student's past experiences and behaviors) to an experiential definition (which ties into each adult's own present attitudes and feelings).

One of the basic tasks of the adult Bible teacher is to relate each truth communicated in the Word of God to the whole life of the learner. As the meaning of God's truth for me as a whole person is realized, the Spirit of God moves in to bring the now-opened personality into harmony with God.

2. It develops closer relationships. The Bible clearly affirms that spiritual growth is affected by the relationships that exist between members of the body of Christ. As we live together in love, God's Spirit builds us up, working through each one as he has been gifted (Eph 4:11-16). Thus, as the commandment to "love one another" implies, the development of close personal relationships in the class ought to be an important concern.

How do such relationships grow? Put most simply, as we come to know one another as whole persons (with facades removed and hidden feelings and attitudes revealed), God's kind of "one another" love grows. We need to know each other as needy persons in order to bear one another's burdens (Gal 6:2). We need to know one another's weaknesses in order to encourage and stimulate them to overcome (Heb 10:24). We need to know each other as those who fall, in order to forgive and forbear (Col 3:13). We need to know one another's joys in order to rejoice with them (1 Co 12:26). We need to know each other as whole persons in order to develop relationships that are essential to the functioning of the body of Christ.

This is one of the most exciting things about teaching an adult class. As we engage the class in the kind of involvement that is "whole person," the students *do* come to know and love each other. The close relationships of Christian love that are formed bind us together in a common experience of Christ's body.

3. It leads to sharing. This is another way to emphasize what's been said in 1 and 2 above. Meaningful participation is that which progresses toward a sharing by your students of themselves.

Sometimes "involvement" takes a pattern of interaction between students and a teacher (fig. 1), with each comment either directed by or to the teacher. In this kind of involvement, the teacher is the center of things. This is *not* a kind of participation we can call "sharing." Sharing involves interaction between members of the class. The teacher will

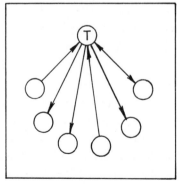

Fig. 1. Teacher as center

be involved, as a participant, but not as the central figure. We might diagram a "sharing kind of participation as in figure

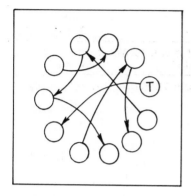

Fig. 2. Teacher as participant

2. This kind of interaction can come, as in the "love" class, by dividing the class into groups of four or more to talk together about something meaningful. Or it can come as a whole class, seated in a circle, talks and listens to one another. But participation that involves interactions between students and students is essential to sharing.

The other dimensions of sharing have already been mentioned. Real sharing involves your students as whole persons. It means that what the class is talking about is not merely ideas, but involves feelings and experiences and attitudes as well.

Sharing will probably take place first in class. But it will soon spill over into the rest of your adults' lives. Right now, my wife has several ladies in our church and class with whom she shares often over the phone, and in contacts during the week. These contacts mean much to her personally: the women share their problems, talk over difficult situations, and so on. They pray for and with each other about specific needs, and they rejoice with each other as God answers prayer.

This kind of relationship is something that will grow out of the adult class if that class helps adults, through mutual participation and involvement, begin to share themselves as they open their lives to the gentle probing of God's Word.

4. It is focused by and around Scripture. Meaningful involvement, as I've suggested before but want to underscore, is built around and brought into focus by the Word of God. The adult Sunday school class *is* for teaching the Bible. Thus the truth to be considered each Sunday will determine

the area of conversation, and the particular kinds of experiences and thoughts that will be shared. We'll look more
at the area of Scripture in our next chapter.

5. *It is spontaneous, not controlled.* This is a word of
caution I want to add. The kind of involvement I've called
meaningful *does* take place in a framework. That framework is a "playing field" with boundaries set by the scripture
passage or doctrine being considered, and with the goal of
whole-person response to the Word. But progress downfield
is *not* under tight control.

To push the analogy, we might say that as in football, a
team can elect to pass or run, and to go to the center or
either side of the field. If the ball carrier gets out of bounds,
play is stopped long enough to get back on the field. And the
team goes back to its task of pushing toward the goal.

It's much like this in teaching adults. As a teacher, you are
not in tight control: the adults have freedom in participation
and will move all over the field, building on and reacting to
what others say in a spontaneous interactive process that no
one can predict or control. But, as a teacher, you *do* define the
playing field. Your teaching plan and the Bible content mark
off the sidelines, and your task is to keep the play in bounds,
and make sure the movement of the group is toward the goal.

Implications of involvement

Meaningful involvement, then, is an essential element in
teaching for transformation. This is not involvement for its
own sake, or that superficial kind of involvement that often
comes as a debate over ideas. Meaningful involvement is
something that grips our students as whole persons, develops
closer personal relationships through sharing, and, while
focused by the Scriptures we are studying, is still a spontaneous thing that helps adults move toward application and
response to God's Word.

If we take seriously the idea that such involvement is

important in teaching adults, then we need to face the following implications.

Implications for the teacher

The stereotype of the adult teacher is of a person who stands behind a lectern and talks to listening students about what the Bible says. He is almost, in this "lecture only" view, a minipreacher.

If we see the adult class as a place where meaningful interaction should take place, we get a very different view of the teacher. He still may lecture. Look over the class transcription again, and you'll note two segments of the class that are definitely lectures—the opening remarks and the extended talk on several of the Bible's behavioral definitions. But the lectures will be planned to stimulate and enrich involvement. They will set the biblical boundaries of the playing field. Rather than being simply an expert in content, the adult teacher becomes an expert in planning and guiding student interaction with the Bible. The teacher of adults has to know *both* Bible content *and* how to help his students discover its meaning for themselves, through involvement.

Implications for the learner

When we see the adult student operating in the kind of class we've been describing, we see a person who is active, who interacts personally with the Bible and tries to grasp what God is saying, who in class, opens up his life to others and shares his feelings and experiences as well as his ideas. The adult is *not* in any sense a passive listener, as he is often forced to be in the lecture-only class.

This role for the adult is strikingly in harmony with Scripture. The Bible insists that every believer is a priest and minister—not just the ordained or sanctioned few. And the Bible also insists that while some men may have a special gift of teaching, *the* Teacher remains the Holy Spirit. This Holy Spirit, who has taken up residence in each believer, will and can teach through all of us.

What an involvement class does then, is to affirm that the human teacher of the class is not *the* teacher, but one of several through whom the Holy Spirit will minister. The class's human teacher is one who works with the Spirit, to free the situation so the Spirit can minister through any or all the class members. Each adult in class, then, becomes a learner/teacher. And participation in the adult class becomes a ministry of one to the other, not simply another way of being ministered to.

Implications for lesson preparation

How will a teacher of adults who seeks meaningful involvement prepare his lesson? While we'll look at details in a later chapter, let's note now that rather than simply determining the points he wants to cover, the adult teacher will plan very carefully the questions he wants to ask and the activities he wants to use to encourage and guide involvement. Teaching for transformation is a very demanding kind of teaching, one that challenges each of us to develop new skills and new understandings. But it is the most rewarding kind of teaching there is. As we help others open up and respond to God, as we hear our students share the transformations God is working in their lives, we experience one of the greatest of thrills that we can know in this life. We see God at work in His people, and know that somehow He used us to touch them.

REACT

1. Here are several possible reactions to what I said in this chapter. Do you feel these actually represent what I said, or not? Why?

   a) "It's a terrible thing to suggest that God never uses lecture. God's Word never fails to accomplish its purpose, does it?"

   b) "I still can't accept the idea that a sharing of ignorance is anywhere near as helpful as a real expert telling what he's discovered in the Bible."

c) "Why, this robs the teacher of all authority! People will get awfully mixed up if they can't have someone step in and tell them what's right."

2. Without rereading the chapter, jot down your own definition of the following key terms. (Check later if you wish to see how they were used.

purposeless involvement
superficial involvement
whole-person
sharing
Scripture-focused
meaningful involvement
spontaneous
interaction

ACT

1. Figure 3 pictures an adult class session as a football field. Think of the class itself as a team. The field boundaries are defined by the Bible truth being taught, and the goal is whole-person response to God's Word.

From what you've learned in this chapter, mark on the playing field the letter of each sentence below to indicate how close you feel each behavior is to reaching the goal of obedience response.

a) The teacher only talks on why people ought to forgive.

b) The teacher exchanges remarks with three of the thirty students.

c) Henry starts talking about life on other planets—again.

Scripture: Eph. 4:32   Subject: forgiving

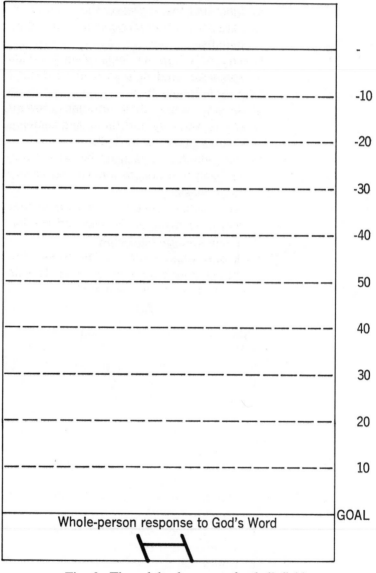

Fig. 3. The adult class as a football field

d) The class discusses together the lexical meaning of forgiveness.

e) Janet and then several others tell of experiences of unforgiveness with their parents.

f) Harv tells how he feels when his kids apologize—and he's so mad he doesn't want to forgive them.

g) Several share their attitudes toward others who may hurt them, and compare these attitudes with God's.

h) Carl tells how God used his wife, Lynn, to teach him how to forgive and accept forgiveness.

i) Several share specific areas where they feel a need for God's help and His forgiving attitude right now.

2. Look over your lesson for **last** week. How might you revise your lesson plan to gain more meaningful involvement?

4

Organizing Scripture

One of the most significant statements of the Bible for the adult class teacher is this: "All Scripture is inspired by God and profitable for teaching, for reproof, for correction, for training in righteousness; that the man of God may be adequate, equipped for every good work" (2 Ti 3:16-17). This is not only an affirmation that the content we teach is truly God's Word; it also teaches that God's Word is purposeful. God's Word is not given merely for information, but that *all of it* may have a teaching, correcting, equipping impact on the believer's life. God's Word is given that we might respond to Him, and in responding, be transformed.

We can hardly justify, then, any classes which teach the Bible *simply* as information. Biblical information is necessary, of course. But we are to move beyond information to relate truth to our lives—and move beyond even this to respond with that active godliness that transformation entails.

So, as teachers of adults, you and I have a multiple task. We must teach the Bible so that it can be understood. We must teach the Bible so that its implications for life are clearly seen. *And* we must teach the Bible in such a way that an obedient response to God is encouraged. The goal of our teaching is always to be our students' response to God, either a short term goal of response from this class, or a longer term of response from this unit, or this quarter.

The fact that teaching the Word of God requires us to focus on response rather than settle for mastery of content suggests that a teacher cannot spend the whole class hour simply talking about what the Bible says. He has to help his students get down to exploring what the Bible means for life in general, and then help each individual discover what this particular truth means to him. This need tells the teacher much about how to organize and plan his class.

Ways of organizing Scripture

There are a number of ways that teachers tend to organize the content they teach. Some of these ways simply do not permit progression from "meaning," to "meaning for us," to "meaning for me."

Verse by verse

The popular verse-by-verse approach simply takes up where we left off last class, and continues as a running commentary on each verse. When time runs out, the teacher stops with a remark, "We'll take up at verse 41 next week." And class is over.

In the best of such classes, there may be discussion of verses and ideas, and suggestions for application as teachers and students work through the material. But even in the best, there is no plan or goal set by the teacher in terms of overall impact or response. The teacher is not structuring the class around a single truth, or designing the class process to explore meaning and encourage response.

It is peculiar that some are so wedded to the verse-by-verse approach. The Bible was not written in verses. These were added centuries later. To treat as determinative in Bible teaching these artificial and arbitrary divisions made by men is, to put it very bluntly, simply astounding. And impossible to justify.

Disjointed topic

Sometimes, adult classes are organized around topics, such as "prayer" or "the future." This kind of study can be meaningful and helpful if we avoid some of the pitfalls. The major pitfall is a simple one: in providing answers to the questions raised, we may take the Bible verses and thoughts out of context, and thus provide a distorted idea of what God says. This approach to Bible study, called "proof texting," is one that the teacher needs to avoid. It can only be avoided by a careful study of the passage in which a thought or text is found.

Topical studies, then, can be valid and helpful. But disjointed topics are not helpful. Simply pulling verses from here and there without a study of their context can be misleading!

Of course, in topical studies too, our goal should always be kept in mind. And our goal is to move from what we learn, to our lives, and to the response to God that discovered truth invites. Sometimes topical studies, particularly today those on prophecy, can and do become mere intellectual exercises, without a probing to discover what the revelation of the future means in historical and biblical context. God's Word—including the prophetic Word—has a vital impact on our lives and transformation. We are to hear it and hear its relationship to us as whole persons.

Units of thought

This is the method I prefer of organizing Scripture for teaching. I prefer it because, in the vast majority of settings (with the exception of such books as Proverbs), the Bible is *written* in units of thought. God is not sharing disjointed ideas: He is communicating in words that we can understand His revelation of reality. Just as you or I choose to communicate, for clarity's sake, in paragraphs and chapters when we write, so God has communicated in units of thought. These units range in length from a verse or two, to paragraphs, to chapters, to whole books of the Bible. The task of the Bible teacher is to help students explore the meaning of God's Word as He revealed it. To trace His thoughts and understand His revelation best, we need to see and grasp the meaning of those thoughts as units.

For instance, Christ once told a wealthy man who asked what he could do to be assured of eternal life, "Go and sell all you possess, and give it to the poor . . . and come, follow Me" (Mk 10:21, NASB). Does this mean that today we should sell all and give it to the poor? Is this a blanket instruction for all believers? Jesus did say it, and it is in the Bible. But when we look at the verse in its paragraph, we see that Jesus was speaking to a man who wanted to earn salvation, one who had been a "good man" all his life. But Jesus' command to him, and his failure to obey, showed clearly that he had put another god before the Lord. His money! He chose his cash rather than commitment to His God.

In context, this command of Jesus was *not* given to the disciples (nor is such a command *ever* given to believers), and the command had the specific purpose of revealing to a man who thought he was good the fact that he, as all others, actually falls short. Only when we put this and other statements of Scripture in their context within a unit of thought can we understand or teach them, or move to see valid personal implications.

As a teacher of adults, then, I want to organize my class sessions around a single unit of divine thought, that I can carry through from seeing what it means, to seeing what it means for people in general, to seeing what it means for each student individually. My goal in teaching any given class will grow out of what God is saying in the unit of thought I'm dealing with, and what that particular truth means when translated into human experience.

The average units of thought will vary in the number of verses they comprise. Chapter 2 treated just two verses as a

unit of thought, and so they are. Classes referred to in the
first chapter treated Genesis 2 and Genesis 3 as units of
thought. Sometimes entire books have a distinctive context
that makes them a unit, within which everything said must
be interpreted (such as Ecclesiastes). Often units of thought
are simply paragraphs that have relationship to their larger
context but still can stand on their own. The critical thing
for us as teachers, however, is to treat the portion of Scripture that we're teaching as a whole—not as an isolated or
unrelated thought—and when we understand the basic truth
God is communicating, to go on to trace its implications
for life.

Preparing for teaching

The helpful thing about teaching biblical units of thought
is that each unit will have a general truth or principle it communicates. What is the general topic? What is being said
about this topic? Can I sum up what this section teaches?

When you can accurately *sum up* what a paragraph or section teaches, *then* you've isolated the "meaning" of the passage. It's then that you're ready to go on and examine the
"meaning for us" and the "meaning for me" of the passage
in preparation for teaching it.

For instance, we might sum up the meaning of John 13:34-
35 by saying, "Love between Christians is essential." But then
we have to go deeper. We have to discover what "love" means
to us. It's here that looking through the Bible and discovering
that God has actually defined love operationally in the "one
another" passages gives us a clue as to how to proceed in
class. So we plan to have our students define love both lexi-
cally and operationally, and share some of the Bible's operational definitions. But then it's necessary to get to the "meaning to me" level. Here we have to have sharing on a very personal level. Response to God's truth is always a personal
thing, and "meaning to me" is discovered best through this
kind of sharing.

Steps to follow

Preparation for teaching a unit of thought involves three distinct steps.

Discover the meaning of the passage. This is something you and I need to do before we teach: dig into the Word of God, carefully tracing and seeking to understand what God is communicating. When we understand a unit of thought well enough to sum up its teaching in a single sentence, we're ready to move on to the next step of preparation.

Discover the "meaning for us" of the truth taught. This is a broader, general statement of the implications of a truth for believers in general. It shows a number of ways a truth might be applied. For example, the teacher might make a chart of three columns to help prepare his lesson. The first column would be entitled, "Meaning"; the second, "Meaning for us"; the third, "Meaning for me." In each column, he would jot down definitions, applications, verse references, and questions all relating to the unit of thought.

Discover the "meaning for me." The last step in our preparatory study is to personally seek God's guidance as to how He wants you and me to respond—now. This Word that we are to teach is *God's.* We're not simply preparing a lesson. We're listening to Him speak to us. And we too need to respond.

So, as a learner, the teacher asks God to make the Word real to him, experienced in his own life before he teaches it to his students. We'll never be trafficking in unlived truth if, in our own Bible study, we constantly ask God to open up our lives, and if we respond in obedience and faith when His Holy Spirit speaks.

Implications

Another phase of this approach to preparation is to realize its implications for our teaching. The emphasis on dealing with Bible as units of thought helps us to keep the focus on a single goal in our planning and preparation. For instance, the goal or aim for the lesson in chapter 2 might be stated like this: To help my students express Christian love to each other now and during the week. This goal was *not* to help them "understand what love is" or to help them "see what loving means." The goal was to encourage response to Jesus' new commandment—to actually love.

An important implication you may have picked up already is that we need to learn meaning ourselves, think through this meaning as it relates to all of us, and apply its meaning to *me*—all before we teach our class. We must have learned God's Word ourselves, in experience, before we can teach it. There are other implications.

Implications for the teacher. As a teacher, I am not to tell others what to do. I am to be a doer. Thus Christ taught that the disciple, when he is fully taught, will *be like his teacher!* He did *not* say will "know what his teacher knows," but that he will be like him! To this, we add the Bible's constant emphasis on the idea that the leader is an example (see chap. 6).

If I am to be an example of one who is living the truth I teach, then I must live it. I must, in preparation for my teaching, explore God's Word and respond to His Spirit as He reveals its meaning for me.

As I teach, I can no longer see myself as a teller. I must see myself as a doer—as an example.

Implications for the learner. Just as the teacher can no longer be satisfied just to understand what the Bible says, so the learner's attention must be focused on experiencing what the Word says. Thus the class session, or class process, needs to move (just as we moved in studying the Scriptures) from developing an understanding of the passage's meaning, to seeing its general meaning for people, on to seeing its personal and specific "meaning for me."

Our personal Bible study and the class process follow parallel tracks! Both lead beyond information to response.

Implications for curriculum. Understanding the process and its goal gives us real help in choosing curriculum. Should we abandon written curriculums and simply "teach the Bible"? This certainly is one option, and, if a teacher is willing to spend time in the Word and able to develop his own teaching plan, it's probably the best approach. But a curriculum is not a substitute for teacher preparation. It's an aid. If a curriculum deals with Bible content in units of thought, and if teaching suggestions fit the development described here (from "meaning," to "meaning for us," to "meaning for me"), then probably it will be a helpful guide and will encourage the development of a teacher's skills.

But a curriculum which does *not* approach Scripture in the pattern described may be harmful rather than helpful, and may lead to the development of poor teaching habits. What it comes down to is that each adult teacher needs to examine carefully his own materials. But, curriculum or no, an adult teacher is himself called by God to teach for transformation.

It's a calling none of us wants to miss!

REACT

1. The Bible should be taught in such a way that its meaning to individuals is explored. Do you agree or disagree? Why? Can you think of exceptions to this approach?
2. For specific guidance in planning how to move from a general Bible truth to its implications and application, read my book, **Creative Bible Teaching** (Chicago-Moody, 1970). Six chapters give detailed instructions on developing the lesson.

ACT

1. Look over the following passages of Scripture and divide them into units of thought: John 15 and Malachi.
2. Fill in figure 4 for **two** of the passages you selected above as units of thought.

Passage: —————

What does it mean?	What does it mean for people?	What does it mean for me?
(truth or principle)	(general implications)	(my response)

Passage: —————

What does it mean?	What does it mean for people?	What does it mean for me?
(truth or principle)	(general implications)	(my response)

Fig. 4. Sample charts

5

Encouraging Response

One thing that sets teaching for transformation apart is that it seeks to encourage response.

Much of our reading and teaching of the Bible assumes that, if people know and believe God's truth, they will automatically respond to it. But Bible history illustrates how generation after generation heard the Word but refused to obey it. And, Hebrews tells us, this kind of hearing "did not profit them, not being mixed with faith [obedient response]" (Heb. 4:2, KJV).

There is much evidence from the social sciences that belief is often unassociated with attitudes and behavior. That is, a person does not always behave consistently with what he says or thinks he believes! A person believes that fattening foods are bad for him and raise his blood pressure, but he fails to change his eating habits. Most people today accept the surgeon general's conclusion that smoking is a cause of cancer, but the sale and consumption of cigarettes are constantly rising. A person may give wholehearted assent to the idea that the races are equal and should be treated with economic and social justice, yet the same person may become very upset and even angry when a person of another race moves into the home next door. A claim to hold a particular belief may say nothing about inner attitudes or values or behavior.

This same pattern carries over into our beliefs as Christians.

This evening, I was talking with an old friend whom I've come to respect and appreciate over the years. He shared what God had been doing in his life these past months, a work of God that has turned his life around, changed his home and work relationships and his effectiveness as a person. He told how he had become burdened and discouraged and despondent, until finally he had simply turned to God and given up, committing himself to little daily acts of obedience. "I knew all the truths up here," he said, tapping his head. "I had taught them all and counseled people. But I didn't know them inside."

This is what the teacher of the Word of God is concerned with; not just knowing truths "up here," but little steps of daily obedience that permit experience of truth, and lead to knowing God's truth "inside."

If our only concern in teaching were to communicate the Bible as true information to be believed "up here," probably a visualized lecture of content would be the best way to teach, or the use of a programmed learning text, or videotaped classes, such as those on educational TV. But if we realize that simply knowing and believing truths does not automatically bring response, if we are committed to helping people respond with little steps of obedience—then we have to structure our classes to encourage and stimulate such response.

Response

It's probably best to think of response just as my friend came to think of his renewed relationship with the Lord. Response involves little steps of obedience, through which God's truth comes to be experienced. We discover the meaning of a passage of Scripture. We explore to find its meaning for people today. We personalize, seeking the Holy Spirit's guidance in pinpointing its "meaning to me," and we then open up our life and personality to God. We respond to God's Word. And it is then, in responding, that our beliefs are linked to life to produce the attitudes, values, feelings, and behavior that, together, express Christ in the believer's personality and life-style.

As teachers, we have to ask this question: what in the classroom will encourage our adult students not only to see the implications of a truth or belief to their present experience, but also to begin to take those little steps of obedience? There are several factors we can isolate.

Seeing the implications of truth

Seeing the implications of truth is a necessary first step. We explore together what a studied truth means in human experience. We study Christ's command to love. In order for that study to issue in obedient response, we need to see *how* love is expressed in our personal relationships. We need to look into Scripture and see the *critical ways* of expressing love that the Bible stresses.

To see implications of the Bible's exciting teaching that we are made in God's image, we need to hear from people like Joan, who have found it impossible to accept themselves or view themselves as special. We need to hear fellows, like Ray, share how their lives have been shaped by the feeling that they have to prove themselves constantly, over and over again. Against this background, we need to affirm what God says: that each of us is valued and worthwhile, because we are persons made in God's image, and important to the Lord. Seeing truth, we need to explore implications. How does it make me feel to know that I'm special? How can I feel about myself, knowing that Christ loved me so much He considered me worth dying for? What does it mean to accept myself—not because I'm perfect, but because even as a sinner, God loves me and affirms my worth?

A first step in moving toward response in the classroom is to help people discover together implications of the truth studied. Sometimes we can do this by illustrating from other people's lives and experiences. But soon, we find that we need to share our own lives, and to compare these with God's truth and His ideals. We need to be free to share, that the practical meaning of God's Word might be illustrated and illuminated in and through us all.

Receiving support

As the implications of God's truth are explored and matched against our lives and experiences, one of two things can happen. Either those who share will be criticized and rejected, or they will be accepted and encouraged. (We'll see in the next chapter how to develop a context of positive support and encouragement.) Whatever the particular response is, it will have a decisive impact on motivating future response. If the attitude of the class is one of criticism and rejection, response to God's Word will be discouraged, rather than encouraged, and soon any honest exploration of implications will be abandoned!

If, on the other hand, the attitude toward each other in the class is one of acceptance and love, response to God's Word will be stimulated. What are some of the dynamics of support that motivate those vital steps of obedience?

1. Acceptance. Many people are blocked from actively following Christ by a sense of their own guilt and inadequacy. They feel more and more hopeless and helpless. They can't seem to feel "accepted in the beloved." They can't grasp the fact that God loves *them,* and fully accepts them for Jesus' sake, as they are, and that He is eager to work in their lives to help them become far more than they are now.

However, when we discover that other Christians welcome and accept and value us as we are—knowing our inadequacies and failures and still caring—we're helped to realize the reality of God's love. We're helped to accept ourselves, to not be so burdened by shame because we are not what we feel we ought to be that we can't face the future with faith and optimism. Sensing God's love for us through others is a basic way that we come to value ourselves as God values us and find the encouragement we need to open up our lives to God for His transformation.

2. Example. When adults are free to share what God is doing in their lives, each shares living examples of the reality and power of Christ. Such examples give us confidence that we too can step out in obedience, and that as we respond to Him, God will work in us too.

It's important here to note that only when we're free in our sharing to tell what *we* are can we show how real and vital *Christ* is. This evening, I know it was hard for my friend to share some of the things God has been doing in Him. To explain how greatly God has worked involved confessing how great his own failures had been! To tell about the little daily steps of obedience to God that have turned his life around, meant to admit that somehow his knowledge of the Word, though he is a teacher of the Word, had been an intellectual and faulty thing. Such admissions are hard for us to make. We're not sure how others will feel. Will they still accept us? Will they still respect and value us? How will they react?

How exciting it is when, in Christian fellowship, we learn that we actually can accept one another and love each other as we are. We can share who we are, and in sharing, we discover how great our God is. What an example this gives, and what encouragement! Others are inadequate, just like me. Yet Jesus has worked in them, to help them live beyond themselves. And in hearing of His work, I realize that He can work even in me. And so we take that first of many steps of obedience that leads to transformation!

3. Encouragement. A third kind of support is received from others in the adult class when sharing takes place. Others ask us how life is going. Others pray for us. Others share similar experiences, and tell how God has met them. Members call one another during the week to share, or communicate prayer requests, or to ask advice, or talk over a problem.

Through it all, we come to realize that there are other peo-

ple who care deeply about us as individuals. There are others
who are eager for us to experience the reality of God's Word
and sense His daily touch. This expressed caring and concern
is encouragement—a unique motivation to step out in trust
and obedience to the Lord and His Word.

Trusting God

The element of trusting God is deeply involved in both the
factors noted above. As we read the Bible, we become aware
of how great a gap exists between what we experience and
what God wants for us. Awareness of this gap can be totally
discouraging and lead us to give up, to simply stop trying, or
to try harder and harder and become more and more frustrat-
ed as failure piles upon failure.

But the Bible warns us that we are to expect just this from
ourselves: total failure. Jesus said, "Without me, ye can do
nothing" (Jn 15:5, KJV). The gap is not something God expects *us* to overcome. The gap is something *He* promises to
overcome in us!

So while apart from Jesus we can do nothing, *with* Him all
things are possible! The Bible then becomes an exciting invi-
tation to step out in faith and *as we obey,* discover Jesus doing in us what we could never do in ourselves. Both the example given as others share what He is doing in their lives and
the encouragement we give one another to step out and trust
God, are possible only because we can in fact trust Him. God
is trustworthy, and He *will* do it. In the atmosphere of love
and sharing that can develop in the adult class, a vital obedi-
ence-motivating confidence and trust in God will grow.

Relationships between critical elements

In this chapter, then, I've suggested that in the context of
fellowship, individuals will be moved to respond to God's
truth. The kind and depth of personal relationships that exist
in the adult class are vitally important when teaching for
transformation.

In earlier chapters, we've looked at the way Scripture is treated and organized, and the kind of participation adults are to be involved in. Figure 5 shows the relationship between these elements in the adult class and also gives us some helpful ways of evaluating where an adult class is.

Level 1 classes

Level 1 classes characteristically treat the Bible primarily as information, and nearly all class time is spent in a study of what the passage means. Usually, there is little student involvement. Where there is involvement, the talk is of ideas and concepts and not of the speaker's inner states or experiences. Relationships in this class are superficial: the adults do not know each other well or come to know each other in the class process. Level 1 classes, which are also characteristically teacher- or lecture-dominated, are the least effective in achieving transformation.

Level 2 classes

Level 2 classes are characterized by greater involvement than Level 1 classes. Talk often focuses on the general implications of the Bible for life. But usually this discussion is in terms of other people, or, when personal, tends to reveal past rather than present experiences. While there is an element of sharing, there is no deep sense of involvement in each others' lives *now*. The relationships in Level 2 classes are often felt to be satisfactory. Class members accept each other, enjoy each other's company, and generally feel comfortable with each other. Yet there is a depth of fellowship that has not been probed. Level 2 classes are more effective in facilitating transformation than Level 1 classes. But the tremendous dynamic of Word and body relationship has not yet been tapped.

Level 3 classes

Level 3 classes are those in which constant, visible transformation *is* taking place. The class is a deeply personal one, with free sharing of present experiences, and discussion of the

	Level 1 classes	Level 2 classes	Level 3 classes
PRESENTS BIBLE AS:	Information	Relevant to life in general	God speaking to me—now
CONCERN	Understanding (What does it mean?)	General implications (What does it mean for us?)	Response (What does it mean for me?)
INVOLVEMENT	Talk of concepts, ideas	Talk of past experiences	Talk of present Experiences as whole person
RELATION-SHIPS	Nil	Acceptance; some sharing of past experiences	Love; depth sharing of present experiences, feelings, attitudes

Fig. 5. How to evaluate the level of a class

relationship of Bible truths to each individual. Present feelings, attitudes, and behaviors are shared, and the class members feel *loved* rather than simply accepted by each other. This class is markedly different from the Level 1 class, in that the teacher is not dominant or in overt control. He is a member of the class, setting boundaries and guiding discussion, but seeking ways to help the students become teachers of each other as they share their experiences with Christ and their insights into His Word.

When an adult class is characterized by Level 3 elements, teaching for transformation is taking place.

REACT

1. Think of your own experience as a Christian. What has most stimulated you to respond to God and His Word? Or, what kinds of encouragement and stimulation do you feel you need most?
2. Can you think of additional things that might encourage people to respond to God's Word in daily steps of obedience?

ACT

1. On the chart of class levels, mark the boxes that most closely describe what is happening now in your adult class. What conclusions do you draw from the pattern you see?
2. Thinking through the elements discussed in these chapters on principles (participation, organization of Scripture, factors encouraging response), what areas do you see of most significance for your own class?
3. Before you go on in this book, write down carefully thought out goals, stating what you would like to see the Lord do in your class during the next six months.

Part 2
SKILLS

6

Developing Classroom Atmosphere

As we've seen in the last few chapters, the climate of the classroom is of critical importance. If there is a sense of warmth, of concern for one another, of acceptance of individuals as they are, then your students will feel free to become involved in meaningful discussion and sharing. But if the climate is cold or superficial, if people do not sense a warm and honest interest in themselves and their contributions, they'll hold back. They'll be afraid to become involved in the significant and intimate way that's necessary as we probe the Scripture's "meaning for us" and "meaning for me."

A cold climate is the primary reason people do not become participants in the adult class, even when asked to do so. Somehow they don't feel that they and their contributions will be accepted, so they hang back. Usually when a teacher complains that "my students don't want to participate," he's making a revealing statement about the climate of his class. In that class, for some reason, adults do not feel accepted. Somehow they do not feel free to share.

Sometimes classroom climate is a reflection of the climate of the church as a whole. Yet it remains true that, in the long run, the teacher sets the climate of his class. So we need to explore some of the things that the teacher does to set climate, and particularly, we need to become sensitive to the little things that communicate to people a sense of being valued.

A spiritual leader

In suggesting that the teacher controls the tone of the classroom, I'm repeating something the Bible asserts in many ways. God has called and chosen leaders for His church: people who are to take the lead and provide an example for others to follow.

I noted this in an earlier chapter. The spiritual leader is charged with teaching the Word of God—and paying attention to his life. The spiritual leader is not to be a little tin god who lords it over the flock entrusted to him, but rather is to be an "example of Christian living" (1 Pe 5:1-5, Phillips). Over and over, Paul reminds the churches to follow the example he provides as He follows Christ. "Those things, which ye have both learned . . . and heard, and seen in me, do: and the God of peace shall be with you" (Phil 4:9, KJV) is what he told the Philippians.

Underlying this strain of New Testament teaching is a simple, yet utterly basic, concept. The taught Word is also to be demonstrated. God's Word is to be heard *and seen* incarnate in the living flesh and blood of the one who teaches it.

What this means for us in our teaching is clear—and jolting. Do you want to see others in your class share their burdens and their joys? *Then you have to take the lead in sharing!* Do you want the members of your class to care about what's happening in each other's lives? *Then you have to take the lead in listening and caring!* Do you want others to feel free to participate and to feel that their contributions are valued? *Then you have to take the lead in showing appreciation!* Do you want to see your students accept responsibility as coministers of the Word of God with you? *Then you have to take the lead in encouraging them—and being taught!*

Whatever characteristics or needs you see in your students, ask God to make those qualities real in you, that your adults may follow your lead.

All this focuses attention on a critical question. What *is* your attitude toward your students? Do you see yourself as "in control," as some kind of authority who is speaking down to those who have not yet come up to your level of spiritual attainment? Or do you see yourself as essentially just another brother, with a special God-given responsibility, of course, but still one called to look on others as better than yourself (Phil 2), and who has the same attitude as the apostle Paul, eager to teach and "impart some spiritual gift," yet quick to note, "that we might be mutually encouraged by each other's faith?" It is this *attitude of mutuality* that, if present, will come through as a real and honest desire for our adults to be meaningfully involved in a shared study of God's Word.

So how about it? Have you developed an honest appreciation for your adults? Do you have a desire to be taught by them as well as to teach them? No "skills" or "methods" can ever substitute for a God-given desire to take the lead in loving, building, and being built up in the Lord.

Communicators of warmth

Normally, the underlying attitude of a teacher will communicate itself as the kind of warmth and interest that builds classroom climate. Yet even the best intentioned teacher may develop habits in teaching that are seen by his students as a desire for distance and status rather than for intimacy and mutuality.

I had a chance to speak with youth sponsors in Detroit this spring on the little things we do that set the tone of a relation with youth, often without even being aware of what we are doing. Afterward, a thirty-year-old came up to talk. "You've just solved my problem." He then went on to tell how he'd gotten along with the church teens as a counselor at retreats and camps. He'd related so well that he was asked to become superintendent in the high school Sunday school department. He did—and everything changed. The kids who had been so eager to stand around and talk with him were respectful now—but not friendly. And he was totally unhappy in the job. What he'd enjoyed most and had somehow lost was a close relationship with the kids, within which he could minister.

I asked what it was that had solved his problem. He said it was the sudden realization that *little things* set the tone of relationships. He had begun to think of what was *different* now that he was superintendent, and pinpointed two things. He himself had been a little insecure and felt that somehow there ought to be respect shown for his position. And the kids stopped calling him by his first name and had begun to use *Mister*. That use of *Mister* was their way of testing to see if he still saw himself primarily as their friend—or if he now saw himself as their superintendent. He let them call him Mister, thinking it was a mark of respect for the office rather than a test of whether he still wanted to be a friend. The kids had misunderstood his motives and had retreated to the safe and superficial relationship of "respect."

What are similar "little things" that may be taken by our adults as a teacher's desire to operate in a cold or formal and impersonal climate?

Name. As with teens, the form of address in the adult class is one tone-setter. If you are known as "Mister," and address your students that way, your adults will certainly hesitate to move toward intimacy.

Seating. Your classroom, its seating plan, and your own physical position when you teach are also important. Formal, row on row seating cuts down eye contact and interaction between adults. It's much more conducive to participation to have students seated in a circle, where each can see and sense a closer relationship with others. In this way too, to communicate to students that you are "with" them rather than "over" them, it's helpful to take a seat in the circle rather than stand behind a lectern. I find that when I have material to lecture, it's best for me to stand up and use a chalkboard. But whenever there is a time for student involvement, I sit down in the circle with them. I try never to have a lectern or table or platform between me and my class members. I want to feel close to them, and such furniture breaks the feeling of closeness that I want my students to develop.

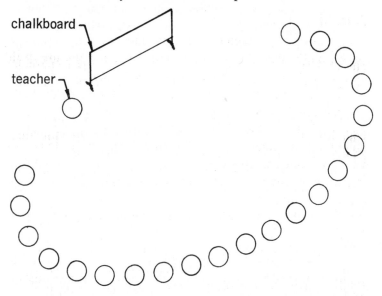

Inviting questions. Often teachers will ask questions that make others feel used or afraid to respond. "Right answer" questions do this to people. In a "right answer" question, the teacher is actually asking his adults to guess at something he has already in mind. "Can you tell me the three reasons why John the Baptist was so greatly used by God?" That little word, *the,* in the question is a dead giveaway. This teacher has already made up his mind about the three. What he's asking is that students guess at his thoughts—and risk being told, "No, that's not quite right," when they come up with an insight that differs from his.

Whenever adults must risk this much to answer or respond, they will very naturally hesitate to participate.

Asking questions about simple facts that anyone can find in the text will also cut down adults' willingness to participate. "How many fish in the nets, according to John 21?" is hardly asking your adults to become *significantly* involved!

So it is much better to ask an inviting question—a question that shows a real concern to know what your adults are thinking and feeling. This kind of question will invite, and result in, involvement. There will be no "wrong" or insignificant answers called for.

Simply put, this means that in teaching the Bible, we want to focus our questioning and our involvement on the "what does it mean for us" and the "what does it mean to me" elements and concerns. It is here that nearly every answer a person can give will be both right (because there are multiple right answers) and significant (because answering will involve some kind of sharing about himself and his perceptions). Look over the questions in chapter 2 again.

Intent listening. Often, a teacher will be too busy thinking of what he plans to say next to really listen when a student is contributing. Intent listening—leaning forward to hear, nodding encouragement, responding with facial expressions to what another is saying, will communicate to adults that what they have to share is important to you. When they sense that you *do* care about what they think and feel, they'll feel free to participate.

Showing appreciation. The nonverbal things noted above communicate appreciation. But the teacher should also verbally express appreciation, both to individuals and to the class as a whole. I find that several times during a class session, I feel a contribution has been particularly valuable, and I say so to the person making it. I also find that after class, there are usually one or two people I want to chat with as we walk to church, just to tell them how much I appreciated something they shared which I personally profited from. More than once, as class has come to a close, I've shared how much I appreciate the willingness of the group to become so meaningfully involved.

Avoiding defensive reactions. Not long ago, I visited a class in which a student saw something in the text the teacher had not noticed or mentioned. When she had a chance, she raised her hand and expressed her observation. Rather than accepting what she said, the teacher launched immediately into a long and involved explanation as to why he hadn't said it himself! In the process of the explanation, he implied first that she had missed *his* point, and then that the point she was making wasn't important anyway!

The teacher had not been attacked, but he reacted as if he had been. No wonder hardly anyone in that class contributed—even when invited to with a halfhearted, "Does anyone want to add anything?" with five minutes left.

Let's remember as you and I teach the Bible, that the Holy Spirit truly *is* the Teacher. He is eager to teach us through one another; He is even eager to teach me through an adult student who may know less about the Bible than I do!

Now, all of the things actually involve one critical element. Always treat your adult students with the respect, consideration, and concern that every person deserves. By seeking to communicate warmth, by looking at our adults with that love that Jesus commands, by acting toward them in loving and considerate ways, you *will* be able to develop the kind of classroom climate in which real sharing and meaningful involvement take place.

REACT

1. Choose one word that best describes the climate of your present class.
2. Look carefully over the "communicators of warmth" described in this chapter. Can you relate the climate, as you have just described it, to the presence or absence of certain communicators?

ACT

1. Describe as thoroughly as possible your own feelings about your students and about your role as a teacher. Then follow through by examining the following Bible passages: 1 Th 2; Eph 4. What insights do these give you about who you are, and should be, as a teacher?

2. If you really want to involve your students in the kind of participation described in this book, why not put the following chart on the chalkboard this Sunday, and explain the class process you want to involve them in? Build your remarks around the discussion in chapter 4.

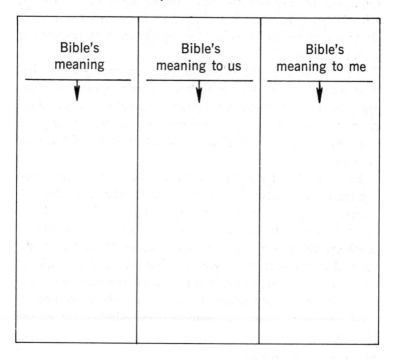

Bible's meaning ↓	Bible's meaning to us ↓	Bible's meaning to me ↓

7

Communicating Bible Content

I've underscored it often. What we are concerned with in this book is teaching the Bible for transformation. That transformation comes only as we grasp the truths of the Word of God and, in response to Him, commit ourselves to live by what He says. Involvement alone does not transform anyone. What transforms is God the Holy Spirit, creating response in us through the Word.

The unique contribution of the kind of meaningful involvement we've been thinking of is that it helps us go beyond dealing with Bible truths as information, and helps us relate those truths to our lives and our total personalities. But clearly, we must have truth to relate! In the adult class, the Bible must be taught.

So we need to ask about the skills involved in communicating the Bible content so as to be clearly understood, that our understanding of a Bible truth may provide a solid foundation for application. In chapter 4, we saw that the best way to teach the Bible is to teach its units of thought as they're developed in the text itself. We saw that we need to work for an ability to express clearly, in a single summarizing statement, the main truth taught in such a unit. Now we need to think about ways to communicate that same truth to our students.

The lecture method

Earlier, I criticized the "lecture only" class quite strongly,

But I do not mean to suggest that a Bible teacher should never lecture. A well-planned and organized lecture remains the fastest way to communicate a block of content and, in many cases, is also the best way. But lectures do need to be well planned and organized! Don't just get up with a few notes and begin to talk! What are the characteristics of a good lecture?

Selectivity

A good lecturer is selective and does not try to cover every detail of a passage. He does not go deeply into words and phrases unless the information is necessary to understand the whole. The Bible is a very rich Book. Every section has an inexaustible store of insights and enrichment. So it's foolish to try to "exhaust" a passage in a single study.

Instead, a good lecturer picks out points for emphasis that make a direct contribution to the basic thesis of that unit of Bible thought. By keeping the focus on the major thrust of the passage, he helps students understand the primary meaning and avoid misunderstandings. This is important; for it is on the primary meaning, the primary teaching (not some interesting but unrelated point), that your adults' exploration of the meaning for them is to be based.

Organization

It's very important in a lecture to have your comments well organized, so that your students can follow what you are saying as easily as possible. I always try to have a short statement of each point written out beforehand, and I usually put it on the chalkboard so that the lecture portion of a lesson can be followed more easily.

If you cannot write down short statements of the points you want to make in a lecture, you probably don't know the passage well enough yourself! This is an indication that you need to dig into the Word some more, to sharpen your own understanding before you attempt to teach others.

Visual Aid

Any lecture is made easier to follow by illustrations used to convey meaning. These may be verbal illustrations (such as the references in Chap. 2 to the experience with church greeters, or the grad student's experience of encouragement). Or they may be visual. An outline of your talk on the chalkboard is one visual aid, so is a simple sketch with stick figures to demonstrate a point. Such things give a lecture concreteness, and make the truths taught easier to grasp.

Function

Since the lecture segment of the lesson is always a part, never the whole, of the class process, it needs to be carefully related to that whole. Usually, the lecture segment will come during the early part of a class session. It will be long enough to provide clear understanding of the text, yet short enough to give the class time to move on to in-depth discussion and sharing. In planning a lecture, then, we always need to think in terms of our *use* of the content we develop. Part and parcel of preparing a lecture is planning the questions we'll ask or the methods we'll use to go from that content presentation to meaningful involvement. The lecture usually fits under the first of the three elements, the "meaning" of a unit of thought. Then it should lead into "meaning to us" and "meaning to me."

Direct Bible study

While lecture is a method most of us will use frequently, we should also be quick to use other approaches to communicating content. One alternative to lecture is in-class direct Bible study. I mentioned using this method in some of my classes described in chapter 1. After taking several minutes to set the stage for study (summarizing the thrust and teaching of the passage is often helpful here), I asked students to read a passage individually, looking for answers to specific questions which I wrote on the board for them.

It's important when you use direct Bible study to give this

kind of guidance. "What evidences do you see of God's care in meeting Adam's needs?" "How do these show God's love for Adam?" Such questions keep the students' thoughts in focus, and avoid having the class become sidetracked by some possibly interesting but irrelevant topic.

Note one important thing about direct Bible study. When you use this method to communicate content, you'll want to include two kinds of questions: questions that deal specifically with understanding the text, and questions that start your class thinking about meaning. Including type two questions will help keep your students on the topic, and will help them learn how to study the Bible for themselves. They'll learn that when we come to the Word of God, we must *always* probe both for what God is saying and for what it means to us. These two types of questions could be used in the "meaning" and "meaning for us" sections of the lesson. When you seek to communicate content by direct Bible study, both types of questions to guide their thinking and thus involve your students both in probing for the "meaning" of the passage and for its "meaning to us."

Preclass study

A third approach to communicating content is to involve your students in preclass study. In this approach, you will provide Bible study guides that include questions dealing with all three class processes (discovering "meaning," thinking of "meaning for us," and of "meaning for me"). This is the most exciting approach, because it permits the adult student to make firsthand discovery of new truths in God's Word, and permits use of nearly all of class time for discussion and sharing.

Here are two sample study guides that we've used in a small group that meets for Bible study and sharing in our neighborhood. Note that all three elements are present, and that the questions help a student dig out the meaning and then go on to apply it.

Ephesians
I. God's Involvement in Salvation
   A. Eph 1:1-14—What God has done for us
   B. Eph 1:15-22—What God is doing in us
II. Our "Contribution" to Salvation
   A. Eph 2:1-10—Past/present contrasts
III. The Nature of the New
   A. Eph 2:11-22—Unity from antagonisms
   B. Eph 3:1-13—The hidden plan revealed
   C. Eph 3:14—4:6—New "possibilities" for us
   D. Eph. 4:7-16—How can we grow?
   E. Eph 4:17-25—A new mind and nature
   F. Eph 4:25—5:2—A new way to live with others
IV. The Practice of New Life
   A. Eph 5:3-20—Pleasing to God
   B. Eph 5:21-23—Submitting to one another
   C. Eph 6:1-9—Accepting responsibilities
   D. Eph 6:10-20—Standing firm, fully equipped

Study 1

Eph 1:1-4—What God Has Done for Us

1. List the verbs in Eph 1:3-14 that tell what God has done in providing salvation, and beside each, give a synonym which seems to you to best restate the idea.
2. Record which of these activities best communicates to you a sense of God's love for you. Why?
3. Select from this passage several verses that form a unit of thought, and paraphrase them. (You may wish to select a section that seems difficult to you, or one that seems particularly meaningful.)
4. Select one or more reasons given in the text for God's actions (e.g., v. 4b), and be prepared to share how that purpose is being realized in your life this week.

Study 2

Eph 2:1-10—Our "Contribution" to Salvation

1. Before reading the passage, list character traits or habits of yours that have in the past, or that presently, disturb you.

2. Eph 2:1-7 gives a "before and after" portrait of the believer.

First, paraphrase vv. 1-3.

Second, complete the chart below, contrasting the description of persons before and after conversion.

before conversion (vv. 1-5)	after conversion (vv. 4-7)

Third, what is the relationship between the characteristics you recorded in question 1 above and the "before conversion" description of persons?

3. Read vv. 8-10 carefully and record your answers to the following questions.

First, what do you think is the most important teaching given here?

Second, what do you think is the most important to you in your own relationship with God?

Third, if there is anything disturbing to you about these verses, what is it?

Fourth, if there is anything encouraging to you about these verses, what?

Extra: If you want to do extra study, why not use a concordance and explore the Bible's teachings on "good works" and on "faith," and on the relationship between the two?

Usually this kind of class study demands a high level of

dedication and a very regular attendance in Sunday school on the part of the adult students. For this reason, few classes take this approach, although increasingly small, home Bible study groups do. It is, however, possible to do this in Sunday school when deeper levels of intimacy and commitment have been reached.

For most classes, particularly those beginning their journey toward more effective transformation teaching, a combination of the lecture and in-class direct Bible study approaches will be best.

REACT

1. If you had to suggest **ideal** time allocations for the three elements that should be happening in your adult class, how would you divide your class time? Fill in on the blanks below.

    Meaning: . . . . minutes
    Meaning for us: . . . . . minutes
    Meaning for me: . . . . minutes

2. Which do you believe is harder for most adults: to understand what the Bible says, or to come to see general implications and respond to what the Bible means "for me"? How is your answer to this question reflected in the time allocations above?

ACT

1. Look over next week's Sunday school lesson and plan a lecture to fit the time you've allocated. Also, plan the transition questions or activities that will help your students move to the next steps in the lesson.

2. Using the same lesson, plan questions to guide your adults in a direct Bible study approach. Then use either of these two plans, depending on which you feel most comfortable with.

8

Methods to Focus Participation

So far, we've looked at two areas of skill that are involved in teaching for transformation. In chapter 6, we saw that the teacher's attitude in class is critical in developing the classroom climate, and that there are many little ways that an adult teacher will encourage or discourage the sharing and involvement that are so critical in transformation teaching.

In chapter 7, I suggested three basic approaches to communicating the biblical content on which all involvement must be based. We are to teach, to learn, and to respond in obedience to God's Word.

Now we shall see some of the important considerations for a teacher who seeks to stimulate and guide student involvement.

Whole-person involvement

The methods that we use to encourage and stimulate involvement need to tap the inner states of our students as well as their ideas. Remember how in the class on love, each adult was asked to share with three others how he had experienced love? In this kind of sharing, he *had* to get below the surface of life, stop dealing with love simply as an idea, and begin to relate it to his own experiences.

The methods for getting below the surface are nearly infinite. But basic to them all are these common factors:

1. They encourage dealing with feelings and attitudes as well as concepts.
2. They help the learner identify his own feelings and attitudes and recall personal experiences.
3. They help the learner relate his experiences to the Scripture, or relate the Scripture to his experiences.

What are some of the methods we might use to do these things? Let's think again about the class transcribed in chapter 2. Figure 6 is a chart of the class, showing something of its progression and the reasons behind each activity, as well as how they fit into the framework I've suggested in this book.

Actually, it's possible to go through this same class and substitute other methods for focusing the same kind of participation at each participation point! For example, here are some of the methods that might have been used instead of those that were.

Launching

"Think of the last time you felt really loved and cared for. Now, tell me one word that says how important that love is to you." Then, move into the lecture by pointing out what Jesus says about love and how we can have a growing experience of love.

Lexical definition

List several definitions on the chalkboard from the dictionary. Ask pairs to discuss whether these adequately explain love. If not, why? If so, how?

Operational definition

"Share in groups of four at least two ways that you personally can tell that another person loves you." Then, hear reports; list answers on the board. Move into the discussion of biblical behavioral definitions.

Experiential definition

"Think of some object you associate with an experience of being loved that is very real to you. For instance, the bedroom

Element	Time	Activity	Purpose
Launch	2 min.	Students tell someone "God loves you"	To start with a positive, warm expression to another person
Meaning	5 min.	Teacher lectures on Jn 13:34-35	To give framework on importance and uniqueness of Christian love
	6 min.	Students (in twos) give lexical definitions of love	To involve students in non-threatening participation
Meaning for us	7 min.	Students (in twos) give operational definitions of love	To begin to probe personal (past) experiences and relate truth to life
	8 min.	Teacher lectures on Bible's operational definitions of love	To communicate "critical behaviors" that show how intensely personal and real Christian love should be
	8 min.	Students (in fours) give experiential definitions of love	To share on a deeper level and to develop some level of trust in preparation for the culminating activity
Meaning to me	5-7 min.	Students (in fours) share love needs and pray for each other	To help act on Scripture in sharing needs, accepting and supporting each other, and expressing love in prayer; to give an opportunity to respond in a meaningful way; to express love—now

Fig. 6. Chart of class transcribed in chap. 2

door in my parents' home, that they left open a crack so I could listen to Mom reading the Saturday Evening Post aloud. Share this object with the other three, and tell how it communicated love to you."

Sharing love-need

Tell of Jesus touching the leper, knowing how much he needed to feel loved as well as to be healed. Ask, "Where do you most feel a need for Jesus' touch today, communicating love for you?" Have students share in groups of four and join hands to pray for each other.

In glancing at this alternate class, it should be clear that the method always has to fit the goal and purpose of each stage of the lesson. Also, a method need not be fancy.

Of course, you can use any number of methods: role play, buzz group, pantomime, debate, reports, analysis, and so on. But the primary criterion for whatever you do in class remains the same. Your method must be suited to helping your adults get below the surface of life, and must fit within the overall class process.

The class process

So far, we've looked at three elements of the class process. Now we want to add a fourth element; in the other Effective Teaching series books, I've called this element the Hook. Simply put, as you launch the study, you will want to touch the pulse of your adults and help them feel that what is to be studied has a vital relationship to them. In figure 6, this element is called the Launch.

Several of the following pages are taken from *Creative Bible Teaching* (excerpts from pp. 228-273), where I explain this process and show that many different methods can be used to focus and guide involvement. What is critical is the purpose of each activity, and its role in the overall process. That process is given these code words in *Creative Bible Teaching*: lesson launching is called Hook; scripture meaning is called

Book; meaning for us is called Look; and meaning for me is called Took. Within the same framework, then, here are ways that the study of a book like Malachi might be developed, expanding the process even beyond one lesson to a unit of lessons.

Malachi

This short four-chapter book concludes the Old Testament canon. It pictures God's people settled down again in indifference to Him, even though just a short half century has passed since the rebuilding of the walls of Jerusalem under the leadership of Nehemiah, marking an end to some of the major effects of the Babylonian captivity—a captivity ordained as a judgment for just the kind of sin and indifference we see reflected in this book!

The book pictures an indifferent society, a company of saints who slipped from coldness toward God into positive rebellion to His ways, while all the time justifying themselves and their behavior.

The book portrays a total pattern of unresponsiveness toward God which is too often characteristic of the life of the church today. And it clearly reveals God, in His character, His motives, His actions, and in His desire toward men who reject Him.

The teaching aim, necessarily a general one because of the complex of possible applications of the book to individuals and congregations today, is to become more responsive to God by evaluating our sensitivity to His will, using criteria revealed in Malachi.

The study of Malachi demands an extended, or unit, approach. The unit developed in these chapters is in eight basic sessions, any of which can be expanded to two or more sessions as the class may desire. The whole unit, visualized in figure 7, expands the Hook, Book, Look, and Took processes and gives one or more whole sessions to each segment of the total learning experience.

MALACHI							
HOOK	BOOK			LOOK			TOOK
1.	2.	3.	4.	5.	6.	7.	8.
Launching	Malachi 1:1—2:9	Malachi 2:1—3:5	Malachi 3:6—4:6	Team	Study	Reports	Response

Fig. 7. STRUCTURE OF THE LEARNING UNIT

In Hook activity options developed in this chapter, far greater creative possibilities exist. And there is room within the structure for the use of several activities, which together focus the learner's awareness of need for this study. All, however, need to help the learner sense a personal need for evaluation—of himself and of the fellowship of which he is a part.

Hook-launching the lesson

In preparation for launching, prepare and display posters of biblical injunctions for self-judgment. Such verses as these may be used: "We shall all stand before the judgment seat of God" (Ro 14:10); "For it is time for judgment to begin with the household of God" (1 Pe 4:17); "Let him who thinks he stands take heed lest he fall" (1 Co 10:12).

The teacher will also need to prepare materials to be used (see suggestions in various approaches, below).

Approach 1. Prepare a slide/tape presentation designed to challenge the group's acceptance of common personal and church practices. The presentation is not designed to *condemn* individuals or the church, but rather to forcefully present the need for critical self-evaluation.

Tape-record a dynamic and impressive reading of Isaiah 1:1-17. Take pictures of a variety of situations in your church and community which will correlate with the passages read. For instance, when verses 11-13 are read, show scenes of your own members at worship, giving their offerings, standing outside the church in "Sunday best," teaching, and so on. Or, with verses 15-17, you might show pictures of the sex magazines at the corner drugstore, composite headlines on youth crime in your community, substandard housing, an orphanage, and so on.

Your group may strongly react to the implication that we and our churches are like the nation Judah which God condemned. Let everyone express himself and argue all he wishes for or against the implied judgment. Then raise the issue of criteria. How do we tell if our worship is an empty show? If our religious habits are just that—habits? How do we know if we're fulfilling our responsibilities as Christ's representatives to those in need? How do we know if our church is?

Conclude the discussion and the session with a brief introduction to the book of Malachi—its historical setting and the fact that, in it, God provides clear guidelines by which we can measure our sensitivity and responsiveness to Him. State the goal for the series: that we all might become more responsive to God by evaluating our present sensitivity to His will, using criteria revealed in Malachi.

Approach 2. Tape-record the following statements for your group to evaluate:

1. "I think I must be the worst Christian that ever lived. I try to do better but—well, to be honest, too many times I don't even try. I don't know why I don't care more about what God wants. It seems that whenever there's a choice to make, I do what appeals to me, without thinking about what He'd like me to do. Maybe it's partly the church's fault. Everyone goes to church and goes through the motions. They sing loud, and bow their heads when the pastor

prays, and look at him when he preaches, but as soon as they're outside, they talk about everything *but* the Lord. I get the feeling that sometimes they just can't wait to get outside.

"But I guess I shouldn't blame them for my failings. I know it's not their fault if I feel so helpless and so useless all the time. It's my fault. I know I can't live up to anything God wants. They just don't come any more worthless than me."

2. "If there's anything that we've got to be proud of in this church, it's the way we go all out for the Lord. Why, look at our missions budget. It's up twenty-three hundred dollars over last year! And we were the highest in our state association then. And we're always out to church for the meetings. The church is full Sunday mornings, Sunday evenings, and even for Wednesday prayer meeting.

"Personally, I'm thrilled to have a place in this church—an important one too. I'm chairman of the finance committee, on the board, and one they always call on when it comes to helping with any problem. My wife teaches Sunday school, and my son is the president of the youth fellowship. And last year my youngest daughter won a week at camp by memorizing Bible verses.

"Now, I'm not proud or anything. I know that the Lord has blessed, and I want to give Him all the credit. But it sure is great to be so blessed, and to know that you're really going all out for God. They just don't come any more dedicated than we are here."

Play both tapes, asking each member of your group to jot down his thoughts after each is played. Give your group a few minutes to compare, in twos, their evaluations of the two monologues. Move then into a general discussion. What seems to be the basic attitude of each individual about himself? About his church? About his relationship with the Lord? On what is this thinking based? How can we tell whether such evaluations are accurate? Throughout the discussion of the above questions, keep a chalkboard list of class ideas, comparisons, and contrasts.

As the group becomes more involved, the class can be divided into smaller buzz groups of four to six individuals to discuss issues like the following: If we were to evaluate our own church, which of the two would we say is *more like* ours? If we were to evaluate ourselves, which person would we be more like? Why? On what criteria did we decide?

One member of each group should keep a listing of the *criteria* by which the members felt individuals and a church might be evaluated. These can be reported to the whole class when the buzz sessions are over. Near the end of the class, the leader should summarize, and introduce the study of Malachi as suggested in approach 1.

Approach 3. In preparation for this unit, select three class members to attempt an evaluation of the general sensitivity of the church and of class members to God's will. Each of the three might be given a separate area of research, roughly paralleling the three areas covered in Malachi: personal relationship with God; commitment to God's standards of concern and righteousness in interpersonal and community relations; demonstrated values and priorities. Each of the three should be free to develop his own ideas. On the launching day, the three can serve on a panel and each report his research and thinking. The panel might then briefly discuss "The Status Quo."

Then involve the whole class in interaction with the panel. Encourage all to express agreement with the panel or to challenge it. After a time of free discussion, lead the group to think of criteria by which such areas might be evaluated. Why is evaluation important? How *do* we know whether we're really sensitive to God's leading or if we've just fallen into a routine and a rut? Near the end of the period, introduce Malachi and the unit.

Approach 4. Give an evaluation form (see fig. 8) to each

member of the group. Encourage each to place both *himself* and your *church* on a continuum scale. When all have finished evaluating, *draw* the form on the board and ask for reports on where the group placed your church in each item.

How Do We Rate?
Place the appropriate sign on each continuous line below, to indicate your evaluation of our church (*o*) and yourself (*x*) in each area.

not honoring God _____	honoring God fully
in-different _____ to God	totally committed to bring Him praise
morally stained _____	living in full holiness
indifferent to injustice _____ around	deeply concerned with justice for all
withholding money, time, _____ and self	fully committing finances, time, self to God
concerned primarily about _____ own well-being	concerned primarily about God's will

Fig. 8: CONTINUUM FOR APPROACH 4

Watch for areas in which there are discrepancies in evaluation. In such cases, ask those who disagree with each other to explain the criteria on which they made their determination. Encourage class discussion through the process of working out a composite evaluation.

When the composite evaluation is completed, ask your

group to say how they *know* the evaluation is accurate? Are the criteria on which they evaluated God's criteria? How does God judge a congregation or an individual? What does He expect?

Near the end of class, introduce Malachi as previously suggested. Be sure to record the class composite evaluation for later use. And encourage each individual to keep his own self-evaluation.

Book—discovering meaning

Remember our general teaching aim: to become more responsive to God by evaluating our sensitivity to His will, using criteria revealed in Malachi. In the basic plan of approach to Malachi (see fig. 7), three separate class sessions are devoted to a study of biblical content. The whole book might be outlined, and the content presentation surveyed as follows:

SEGMENT	SESSION	SOURCE
I. Historical setting	Launching	Collateral readings
II. Relationship with God	1	Malachi 1:1—2:9
III. Relationship with men	2	Malachi 2:10—3:5
IV. Relationship with self	3	Malachi 3:6-15
V. Warning and hope	3	Malachi 3:16—4:6

In summary, Malachi shows that the people of God, even after the judgment of God on their fathers, were now unresponsive and indifferent to Him (II), were uncaring and heedless of others' needs and rights (III), and were completely self-centered in all they did and thought and valued (IV). While the society was thus abandoned by God to judgment, individuals who feared the Lord came together to speak of Him and encourage each other in obedience (V). These were remembered and honored by the God whom they honored; the rest were warned of judgment to come.

The task now is to discover why God judges these people. What are the criteria on which He rejects them? Let's see a number of ways in which our students can become involved (in class or before class) in studying the message of the passage. For brevity's sake, we'll look at the approaches tailored to segment II, Malachi 1:1—2:9.

Approach 1. Give each student a chart (fig. 9), which organizes the passage around the three cynical questions asked God by His people. Have each student study the passage and complete the chart by filling in the blank columns.

Question	God seen as	The appropriate response to God	Their response to God
How have you loved us? (1:2)	loving		
How have we despised	a Father		
Your name? (1:6)	a Master		
How have we polluted Your altar?	Lord of hosts the great King		

Fig. 9. MALACHI CHART

Then discuss in some depth the response God's character called for, and the response these people made, or this may be done by the entire class during your session.

Approach 2. Ask each student to write a two-paragraph summary of the heart of the message of Malachi 1:1—2:9. Compare the summaries and discuss differences. This will drive your students back into the passage to explain their impressions, and it will involve the whole group in a joint effort to locate and clarify the major issues.

Approach 3. Ask each student to read through the passage and place the corresponding letter beside each verse to which it applies:

- *a*) raises a question in his mind
- *b*) tells something about the person of God
- *c*) pictures the thinking or actions of God's people
- *d*) seems to have parallels in modern life

Each should compare those verses beside which symbols *b* and *c* have been placed, to get a clearer picture of what the passage teaches in each area.

Most students will probably question such phrases as "Jacob have I loved, but Esau have I hated" (1:2-3). The teacher will need to explain that this is a common Near Eastern formula used by a father in his will. The word *loved* indicates the one whom the father has chosen to inherit; *hated* indicates a decisive legal rejection of any rival claim. The formula does not necessarily imply animosity or anger, as *hated* does in our culture.

Approach 4. Ask each student to write out a character sketch of God's people as portrayed in Malachi 1:1—2:9 and of God as portrayed in the same passage.

Read several sketches and then discuss the biblical evidence on which these are developed. In what ways was the character of the people evidenced? How is such character manifested today?

Approach 5. Have each student make an analytical outline of the passage. Outlining should point up the major thrust of the passage clearly, and need not be completely accurate to be of great value.

For instance, here is one adult's outline:

Outline of Malachi 1:1-9

I. God's Love for Israel (1:1-5)
   A. God expresses love for Israel (1:2)

    B. Israel questions God's love (1:2)

    C. God demonstrates His love (1:2-5)

        1. God chose Jacob over Esau

        2. God has wasted Esau's country

        3. God will keep on tearing down his country. (Note: it is for their "wickedness," 1:5)

        4. God will keep His people's borders

II. Israel's Dishonoring God (1:6-9)

    A. God says He gets no honor from Israel (1:6)

    B. Israel questions this (1:6)

    C. God proves His point (1:7-8)

        1. Offer of polluted food on the altar

        2. Sacrifice of worthless animals (something they wouldn't dare give to a human governor!)

    D. God refuses to accept their offerings

        1. He is great over all the world

        2. They give of their worst

        3. They are bored with His worship

    E. God warns the priests

        1. He will curse them if they do not give Him glory

        2. They don't really worship or fear God

        3. They don't live uprightly

        4. They have led others astray, away from God

Approach 6. Note that in each of the approaches suggested above, a necessary next step is to relate the failings of God's Old Testament people, together with the criteria God used to judge them, to us today.

While it is true that in the unit approach, most of the Look process (seeking insight into the meaning of the biblical message for twentieth-century life) will take place later in other sessions, some definite attempt to begin that relating process must take place in the Book sessions.

Each of the methods suggested above is easily taken this step further. Two new columns can be added to the chart (fig. 9) in approach 1: "What should *our* response be?" and "What *is* our response?" In other approaches, a shift to modern life is equally easy. In the last approach, for instance, the question can be raised, "If God were writing about us today, what would be His possible evidence under I:C and II:C?"

At the same time, some approaches to content demand both a careful study of the text and a thoughtful attempt to spell out its implications.

One of these is the modern paraphrase. Select one or two significant segments of the passage and ask the students to rewrite them as though they were being spoken to us in America today. For this passage, you might select Malachi 1:6-9, 1:11-13, and perhaps 2:6-9.

Approach 7. Divide your class into three teams, each of which is to present one of the three major sections of Malachi. Ask the team assigned the first section to develop and present a two-part drama, which will portray in the lives of twentieth-century people the characteristics which God condemned in the people of Malachi's day.

One of the team members should lead a general discussion of the drama afterward, showing the parallels between Malachi and modern life that exist and that were dramatically developed.

The challenge to justify or to invalidate the conclusions thus presented will drive the whole group into the text for further study and discussion.

Look—discovering meaning for us

In structuring the unit on Malachi, several options as to arrangement of sessions and learning activities exist.

For instance, it would be possible to organize the unit with a Look session following each content unit, like this:

Launch	Malachi 1.1—2:9	Look	Malachi 2:10—3:5	Look	Malachi 3:6—4:6	Look	Took

Fig. 10. Malachi broken down into content units

Or the unit could be organized to permit a series of Look sessions following a series of content coverage sessions, like this:

Launch	Malachi 1:1—2:9	Malachi 2:10—3:5	Malachi 3:6—4:6	Look			Took

Fig. 11. The Look session following content units

This second option opens up at least two possible approaches. One, the implications of the message of Malachi as a whole can be discussed in the three sessions set apart for guiding to insight. Two, one of the three sessions can be related to each of the three content sessions. It is this approach that is suggested here. Why? Because application of the message of Malachi to today demands a careful investigation of our contemporary church and personal practices. Adequate application to twentieth-century America of Malachi's revelation of God's expectations for His people demands that we get beneath the surface of what is so commonly accepted, and thus so seldom honestly examined.

I noted earlier that we should begin to explore the implications of Malachi as a part of our study of the biblical text. Thus, the methods suggested for communicating content contained questions and activities which encouraged the students to seek parallels in modern life. For a series such as this to be most meaningful to the students, and for it to utilize the factors discussed in chapter 4, some relationship of Malachi to our lives, *now,* should be established in the content segments—although they need not necessarily be *developed* there.

The approach taken in this unit, then, requires that some awareness of the relevance of Malachi be established in the content study itself. And it expects that students who are particularly interested in an aspect of the study will take responsibility for further research.

The relationship of the Book and Look sessions in this unit might be visualized as follows:

Thus the Look process, begun in session 2, will be continued and completed in session 5, with the delay designed to enable a team of class members to examine in some depth practices of our own which Malachi's message may call into question.

Session 1	2	3	4	5	6	7	8
LAUNCHING HOOK	Malachi 1:1—2:9 BOOK ------- LOOK			LOOK (continued and developed)	LOOK	LOOK	TOOK

Fig. 12. The Look sessions separated by content units

Look activities in the content session

When thinking, then, of the Look process, we need to remember that learning activities should be structured for sessions 2, 3, and 4, which will help the group *begin* to explore contemporary questions the Malachi message may raise. What might such activities be?

Approach 1. Add two columns to the chart suggested for approach 1 (fig. 9). One column should be captioned, "What should our response be?" and the other, "What *is* our response?"

As these columns are completed by the class, ask how we can be sure that our practices are not as routinized and unrelated to God's desire for us, as were the practices of Malachi's day.

Approach 2. Tape-record comments of several college youth on Sunday school and church. Young people today tend to be critical of the institutional church. Many feel that we *are* expressing a deadened ritualization like that of the Old Testament.

To stimulate their comments, read Isaiah 1:11-12 and ask a young person whether he feels this might be God's attitude toward the contemporary church. And ask why he feels as he does.

Play the reactions in class. Then ask your students to evaluate. Why do youth feel as they do? Is it possible that we *are,* in some ways at least, like the men of Malachi's day? How?

Approach 3. Ask the class what, if God were writing to us today, He might present to us as evidence of indifference and unresponsiveness to Him.

Approach 4. Incorporate *application* as an integral part of the content covering technique. Note suggestions earlier, under approaches 6 and 7, on creative paraphrase and drama.

Look activities beyond the content session

In none of the approaches suggested above can any firm determination be made, nor can the actual situation be accurately sketched.

In this study, and *in many other Bible studies,* assessment of the implications of the Word for our day and our lives demands in-depth, continuing exploration. In this particular study, let's suppose that several of the class members are concerned about our religious practices, as God was about those of the Israelites (Mal 1:6—2:9). Ask for five or six interested volunteers to look into the area and report back to the class in three weeks. At this point, your role is to help the research team plan how to gather information for the report to the class in the later session. The learning activities they now undertake are *out of class* activities, which, upon report to the class, will stimulate more intelligent discussion in the follow-up session.

How then can the team explore the meaningfulness of our church life and practices?

Approach 1. Provide books and materials on the contemporary church. While much available today is simply critical, some writers attempt to evaluate and give constructive suggestions.

Materials which might be particularly helpful to such a team would include Keith Miller, *Taste of New Wine* (Waco, Tex.: Word, 1965); Walden Howard, *Nine Roads to Renewal* (Waco, Tex.: Word, 1967); Wallace E. Fisher, *From Tradition to Mission* (Nashville, Tenn.: Abingdon, 1965); Larry Richards, NAE study booklet, *Tomorrow's Church,* and others. Have each team member read at least one book or booklet and attempt to relate what is said to the Malachi passage. They should meet together to share their discoveries after one week.

The readings may open up several ways of reporting to the entire class, planned for session 5 of this study. Team members may serve as a panel, to summarize the thrust and ideas of contemporary writers; or quotes from the readings may be reproduced and mailed before class to each class member. The class members can then make comparison criticisms with Malachi 1:6—2:9 as preparation for class discussion.

Approach 2. After reading, the study team may decide that further research is needed. Areas of contemporary church life which are being questioned today may be isolated, and research may be done within their own congregation.

For instance, how effective is the church in reaching others in the community with the gospel? A survey of membership additions (checked whether by conversion or letter) or of recorded results of various agency ministries might be made. Or a spot check of the witnessing by lay members might be taken. Or a questionnaire asking church members to evaluate the contribution of the church to their lives (and giving specific criteria for the evaluation) might be developed and passed out.

Or a study of the youth in the church might be undertaken.

How many drop out of church when they reach high school? Why do they leave? What is the attitude of those who stay on? Do they stay because they *want* to or because they have to? How do the youth evaluate the relevance of the church ministries and activities to their lives?

Information thus gathered may be reported to the class, through charts, verbally, and so on. Thus information needed to correctly assess the implications of Scripture to this particular fellowship can be provided.

Approach 3. The group might attempt to find believers in other churches who are experiencing what Keith Miller calls "the taste of new wine." Or a member of a church that is trying in various ways to make its services and ministries more relevant might be invited to share with the class what has been happening in his church.

Note that all of these approaches are designed to gather information to stimulate further discussion and evaluation of the impact of the Scripture studied. Each presumes that the hour set aside for further discussion will be a *discussion* session, a session in which the study team introduces enough information to make discussion meaningful, to give the group a basis for evaluation of the ideas under consideration.

The easy "Oh, we're all right" and the too quick "Everything today is horribly wrong" are both put to rest when facts replace unreasoned opinion in discussion, when that discussion is an open sharing between group members who are determined to understand and to do God's will as revealed in Scripture and applied under the Spirit's direction to the real situation in which they live.

In this process—this time of examining together the *meaning* of Scripture for us—the basic and ultimate method is discussion.

A quick check over the learning activities suggested in this chapter will demonstrate a significant fact: each is designed to stimulate discussion of the implications of God's Word for *us,* now!

In such discussion, we exercise our spiritual gifts, and we minister to each other, when we say what we really think and believe and feel in full commitment to each other and to the authority of the Word in our lives. In this context of fellowship (Greek, *koinonia,* "sharing"), the Holy Spirit works through each of us to minister to the others, and He leads each of us to a knowledge of His will for our lives. We discover together new, unexpected ways in which God's Word calls us to response to Him. It isn't easy for us to enter into true fellowship with each other. To open up—to ourselves, to others, or even to God.

Took—discovering meaning for me

Like the Look process, the Took in a unit study may begin in any of the sessions. Individuals may hear God's call to them as the Word is studied. Others may see more clearly what He desires as the implications of the Word are explored in the session set aside for that purpose. But a unit study normally demands at least one session of hard, conscious consideration by the group of the question, What must *we* do?

A variety of approaches can be designed to help the group ask and answer that question. Here are some:

Approach 1. Repeat the slide/tape presentation with which the unit was launched. Ask, "How did you react when you first saw this presentation? How do you feel about it now?"

As the learnings of the unit are summarized, challenge the group to define what, in light of the Word of God and the meanings they've discovered it has for them, they must do. What response does God demand of them?

Approach 2. Ask each study team, on the basis of the class discussion of their report, to draw up a series of proposals, attempting to define the action that they feel individuals and the class as a whole ought to take in response to God's Word.

Have each team present its proposals for discussion by the class, for any action the group may decide to take.

Approach 3. Place on the chalkboard the composite evaluation chart (fig. 8) which the class constructed during the unit launching. Ask the group how, after the study, they would now evaluate their congregation. As changes are logged, ask the group to suggest *how* they might move to achieve the goals. What must be done? How might it be done? What role can/should the class play? What is the role of the individual?

In suggesting the above activities, I have apparently presupposed that the Took process is always to be a part of the class session. This, actually, is not necessarily true. Youth and adults need to "learn how to learn" when it comes to studying the Bible. But when the group becomes response-oriented—when the class moves spontaneously into an open discussion of the meaning of the Word for their lives—then special Took activities become less and less necessary. For the group is learning to think response when they come to the Word, and their hearts and minds are opened up to the ministry of the Holy Spirit. At this point, each class member tends to take personal responsibility for doing the Word.

In an open, sharing discussion this sense of personal responsibility *to do* the Word of God, to which the whole group is committed, becomes the primary and only necessary means of creating motivation.

Summing up

Teaching for transformation does involve both philosophy and skills. A teacher of God's Word should both understand the nature of his ministry and grow in his ability to function effectively. The most critical elements of all are these:

Be the kind of person who is an example. Dig into the Word yourself, and ask God to make real to you, as you obey Him daily, those transforming truths you will teach Sundays.

Be the kind of teacher who cares about his students and who is eager to see them transformed. Seek honestly to understand the teaching ministry to which God has called you, that you might not only teach His truth, but teach it His way!

REACT

1. If creative methods seem difficult to you, please get and study the book **Creative Bible Teaching.** It is specifically designed to help you develop skills as a teacher.

ACT

1. Go back to chapter 4, and see if you can develop a lesson plan for one of the passages you studied under the Act section. Try to incorporate all the principles discussed. Then reread each of the last three chapters, with that plan in front of you, checking to see if and how you implement the critical considerations we've discussed. For instance, did the questions you jotted down communicate interest in others' contributions, or were they "right/wrong," or "fact only" questions?

2. When you've been over the lesson plan, teach this lesson on Sunday rather than your regular curriculum.

Part 3
SETTINGS

9

The Graded Class

A number of different approaches to structuring adult classes have been used in the Sunday school. The most common way of forming classes has been by age-grading. Thus we have classes formed for singles, for just-marrieds, for thirties to forties, and so on. Normally such classes go on together for years, with new classes being formed under the existing ones as new generations come into the church. Such classes may start small, but in larger churches soon grow beyond the closely knit original group. Over the years, they may expand to include well over a hundred people. Often too, the same teacher will remain with a class through the years, forming a special attachment with the group.

There has been much recent criticism of the graded class, and many churches have been experimenting with alternative approaches. But there are many advantages to this system too. So in this chapter (and in the chapter to follow), we'll look not so much at problems but at the possibilities for transformation teaching, and to see ways to make the advantages work for you, the teacher.

Advantages

Among the many advantages of this traditional way of grading adults, the following stand out as real aids in teaching for transformation.

Time together. Some approaches to grading break up groups of adults after a relatively short time together. Relationships may begin to develop in these shorter periods, but just as a level of trust and love are being reached, the course is over and the group disperses. The graded class is one that you can expect to be with for a significant period. Even if much time has to be spent in helping students come to a place where they feel free for meaningful involvement, you can have confidence that that time will not be wasted. You will be able to work slowly and lay a foundation for productive months and years of study together.

Often when a class has been together for some time, the pattern of what happens in the classroom is set. If a group has come to Sunday school for years to listen rather than participate, it will take considerable time to change the pattern. In an adult class in a large, Illinois church, it took nearly eight months before the group (about twenty people ages thirty to forty) began to open up and become meaningfully involved. But over the next years, that class maintained an openness and enthusiasm in study and sharing that made it a significant experience for all of us, and led to its growth to one hundred who, even with the unwieldy size, still maintained a healthy level of fellowship. It may take longer to help adults who have been together in a nonparticipation class shift to the kind of involvement needed for transformation teaching, but once the new pattern is set, staying together will help maintain the learning climate.

Social unit. The traditional graded class has been a social unit as well as a study unit. Adult social activities and friendships, particularly in churches where size makes it impossible to know everyone well, have often been built around the class.

Some have objected that this is "breaking up" the church. Actually, it can and should contribute to church unity. No one will know *everyone* well in any church. Yet all need a close and intimate relationship with some. If these relationships are developed within Sunday school class fellowships, the church will be far healthier than if no opportunities are provided for developing and maintaining fellowship.

It is true that in some adult classes, the relationships have remained superficial, and have been "social" rather than spiritual in nature. The fact is, however, that the quality of relationships is determined by what happens during the class hour! If there is the kind of sharing that helps adults come to know one another as real people, to develop concern and to care for one another, and to reveal Christ's working in their lives, then relationships outside the class will also provide deeper fellowship. This does not mean that the social has no place in the class fellowship. It does; believers ought to have fun together and enjoy one another's company. But we do have to be concerned with the deeper levels of fellowship that the Bible describes as part and parcel of our lives with each other. The graded adult class can be a social unit that effectively promotes the experience of fellowship and love within the church.

Similarities. The grouping of graded classes by age also means that people of similar age and common experience will be probing the Scriptures together. This has a definite in-class advantage. Young parents will share common concerns about their marriages, raising their children, their job and economic commitments, et cetera. They will be able to identify with each other and share from their similarities ways that God has been dealing with each.

There are advantages to having fellowship across the ages, of course. But the common ground provided in graded classes is also helpful in focusing sharing on common needs.

Of course, there are also social advantages. A young adult class might choose skiing for an outing—certainly a problem if some grandparents are also members!

Each of these aspects of the graded class is an advantage for both the teacher and the students. There is time in a graded

class to come to know one another well and to develop a
healthy pattern in which all will be comfortable. There is a
base provided for in-class learning and sharing, for coming
to know each other well and setting a tone for fellowship in
the group. There are other similarities that make finding a
common identity easier, and that permit the members to enjoy
similar things together.

Exploiting the advantages

Each of these advantages can become a disadvantage, unless
used wisely by the teacher and students. A class that stays
together for years can get into a rut; a teacher can fall into a
routine. Social activities can become so centered on the class
that others (especially newcomers) are excluded as special
friendships become exclusive and ingrown. Too much similari-
ty can cut a group off from contact with others and understanding of their feelings—building a "generation gap" in the
church! So it is important to realize both the potential of this
grading system, and the possible dangers, and then to work at
exploiting all the advantages. How?

After about a year and a half with my adult class in Illinois,
several couples complained. I had been using a variety of
methods to gain involvement, something very necessary as we
began together, because the group simply did not want to
participate. But later, the pattern of the class (launching,
"meaning," "meaning for us," "meaning for me") had become
clear to all. My adults had learned to think in the framework
of this process. And the methods I was using were no longer
necessary! The class was eager to discuss (*the* basic method
in transformation teaching), and they could go quickly from
what the Bible says to its meaning without methods to help.

To exploit this advantage (my students were now *with* me
in the pattern), I changed. I simply launched class, moved
into a quick study of the content, and then with a mere query,
turned them loose!

As interest grew, I found we needed a way to keep the continuity of our study clear for those who had to miss a Sunday. So I began to send out a weekly newsletter, in which I included two or three questions a couple might talk over about the passage to be studied the next week. Our studies in this way were aligned to the overall context of the book, and also kept in sharp focus.

I also found that giving adults credit by name for their contributions in class helped to communicate to everyone that their involvement was important and a ministry to others. Including a list of prayer requests was another way of saying that we did and could care for each other in practical ways.

The fellowship expressed in the class also carried over into the week. We included newcomers' names and addresses in the newsletter. Every Sunday afternoon, some of the couples would hold a kind of open house, including newcomers and visitors and some of our regulars. Little things like these kept our fellowship open and inclusive, helping protect us against becoming ingrown.

We had many social activities, ranging from a formal dinner to very informal class picnics at a nearby farm, and the children were always included in these—about two hundred all told. There was no effort to make this anything but a fun time. Yet I clearly remember at one of these summer picnics that a young man was led to the Lord. Talking about Jesus was normal and spontaneous. We had grown in our freedom to share in class.

To the extent that meaningful involvement in one another's lives begins to take place in the Sunday school class, the pattern of relationships in Christ set then will carry over into the whole life of the believer.

The graded class, then, is an excellent setting in which teaching for transformation can take place—in *any* graded class.

REACT

1. How much time do you think a teacher ought to be willing to put in to change the pattern and climate of a class that is well established?
2. Or is it better to begin a new class with new people? What are advantages and disadvantages of this approach?

ACT

1. If your class is age-graded, take time to list all the advantages and disadvantages of the system that you have experienced.

10

The Elective Class

The use of elective classes for adult education has many proponents today. Among the advantages suggested are that the short term of the class prevents it from becoming a little church. It also permits selecting teachers to teach subjects in which they have special competence. And it lets adults select from a broad range of topics not covered in other approaches.

It would seem that these advantages do not really contribute to teaching for transformation. However, there are many possibilities to consider in structuring the adult education program of the church. In some of them, the elective approach has strong appeal.

Part of a whole

The first thing to remember is that any class is only a part of the whole program of adult Christian education. Teaching for transformation must be taking place somewhere within that whole—but not necessarily during the Sunday school hour! One pastor noted that only a small group was coming out for the weeknight prayer meeting. He dropped the "sermon" approach and decided to use it as an occasion to teach for transformation. The service became just the kind of "class" I've been describing in this book. Not only did attendance grow, but it also made it possible to use that Sunday morning hour to reach different goals.

In another church, a number of small, home Bible study groups have been formed. The kind of meaningful involvement and sharing focused by Scripture that I've been describing is taking place in these small groups. Again, the Sunday school hour is now available for other purposes. The "transformation need" is being met, and all in the church have the opportunity to become involved in the small groups.

Goals

What are some of the different goals that people might seek to reach during the Sunday school hour?

Content mastery. It is important in applying God's Word to know it well. Many adults are ignorant of the overall structure of the Old and New Testaments and of Bible history. So it is perfectly valid to use the Sunday morning hour to conduct a true "school," to teach for a clear understanding of the Bible basics as a framework within which our personal Bible study might take on deeper meaning.

Social issues. A number of issues face us as Christians who are also members of modern society. These range from questions of ecology and abortion, to topics like missions strategy and poverty. Electives during the Sunday school hour give adults a chance to interact over these issues and discuss their responsibilities.

Christian life. A number of books on subjects like prayer, interpersonal relationships, unity in the church, and so on, are also available in elective structures. Some of these are subjects our members will feel a special interest in and need for.

Others. Many other special topics are open to exploration in elective classes, such as Bible archaeology and prophecy. Some classes today are even involving adults in the study of Greek.

When the need for transformation is being met in Bible study in other settings, all of these possibilities are opened up for that Sunday school morning hour.

Advantages

Flexibility. The elective concept has made it possible to structure Sunday morning education to meet a variety of needs. Are there new believers in the church? Then why not a special new converts class? Are there those who want a deeper, lasting fellowship through the graded approach? Then why not have graded classes for those who want them, and give elective opportunities as well? Does the summer slack period mean that many leave for vacations? Why not stop a graded system then, and offer special one-month elective studies during July and August?

Even smaller churches, without specialized talent to teach a variety of electives, can use this elective approach if they are willing to operate with small groups. Why not plan a study based on one of the many pocket-sized study books, if as many as eight people sign up—and express willingness to teach themselves? Let each read the appropriate chapter before class and be ready to contribute. Or rotate leadership, letting each class member take the leader's guide usually available and lead one session; then rotate leadership to another person.

Selectivity. Selectivity is much like flexibility, except that it emphasizes the freedom of the adults in the church to choose something for which they are ready. In one church, the leaders felt that the fellowship described in this book was needed, and wanted to help adults understand that fellowship, through experiencing it. So the pastor offered a special class, taught to a maximum of ten people, who would commit themselves to be at every session for twelve weeks. He helped them develop the kind of trust and love for each other that marks meaningful involvement. Then when the time was up—although the class begged to continue—he took another group of ten and held another "fellowship training class." Through this process of self-selection, those who felt a need for fellowship training chose to become involved. Others who were not yet ready were not forced into involvement. But as the reports were shared of those who were involved, more and more members of the church requested and received fellowship training.

Thus, the elective structure was actively used to build the kind of relationships that we've been describing in this book that are so basic to Bible study.

Termination. A final advantage of the elective approach is that it does have impermanence built into the system. After a course is over, the group that took it breaks up, to become involved with different people in the next class. In a church where relationships have become ingrown and patterns of grouping have become habitual, an elective system can help expose members to one another and encourage the building of new relationships.

It's not the settings

While both graded and elective systems have advantages and disadvantages, the fact is that it is not the learning settings but what happens within them that counts. At some point in the church program, in some setting, every adult needs the opportunity to study the Bible for transformation. Every adult needs that intimate relationship provided by meaningful involvement.

In many churches, small groups meeting in homes during the week are meeting this need. In others, the Sunday school hour is the only or the best setting. In such a case, it is probably best to seek, in graded classes, to build a group of adults into a living fellowship of men and women who share weekly the meaning of the Bible truths they study together.

And in this setting—in the Sunday school—the nature of the class, its climate, and its effectiveness will be determined by you, the teacher. It will be your decision whether to commit yourself to teaching for transformation, or to teaching for some other goal. The exciting thing to me is that, as a teacher of adults, I know that God's Word is a living Word, and that God's Spirit is present to transform. Because of the Word and the Spirit, I can take the risks involved in teaching for transformation. I can try new things—with faith and confidence. For I know that whatever my inadequacies, as I seek to teach God's Word in God's way, the Holy Spirit who is the Teacher will teach—and *He* will transform.